"A Rough Introduction to This Sunny Land"

Henry A. Strong and his wife, Mary Katherine, 1867.

Photograph courtesy of
Carolyn Gleason and Ralph Moody

"A Rough Introduction to this Sunny Land":

The Civil War Diary of Private Henry A. Strong, Co. K, Twelfth Kansas Infantry

Edited by

Tom Wing

Butler Center for Arkansas Studies
Central Arkansas Library System
2006

BUTLER
CENTER
BOOKS

Butler Center for Arkansas Studies
Central Arkansas Library System
100 Rock Street
Little Rock, Arkansas 72201

Original ISBN: 0-9708574-3-8
Civil War Sesquicentennial Edition ISBN: 978-1-935106-28-9

First published in 2006

Editorial supervision: Brian K. Robertson
Book design: Timothy G. Nutt
Cover design: H. K. Stewart

Library of Congress Catalog Card Number: 2005927878

Strong, Henry A. (Henry Albert), 1845-1927.
    "A rough introduction to this sunny land": the Civil War diary of
Private Henry A. Strong, Co. K, Twelfth Kansas Infantry / edited by Tom
Wing.
    xxii, 96 p. : 23 cm.– (Butler Center Book Series)
    Includes bibliographical references.
    ISBN 0-9708574-3-8
    1. Strong, Henry A. (Henry Albert), 1945-1927. 2. United States.
Army. Kansas, Infantry Regiment, 12th (1862-1865). 3. United States—
History—Civil War, 1861–1865—Personal narratives. 4. Arkansas—
History—Civil War, 1861–1865. I. Wing, Tom.
E508.5 12th .S77 2006
973.781 S —dc

Printed in the United States of America

The paper used in this book complies with the Permanent Paper Standard
issued by the National Information Standards Organization (Z39.48-1984).

This volume is dedicated to
Joe and Shirley Wing,
my parents, who always encouraged my love for history

Contents

List of Illustrations

Foreword

Early in June 2002, I received a telephone call from Tom Wing, a park ranger at Fort Smith National Historic Site. He informed me that he had transcribed and edited the Civil War journal of Private Henry Strong for publication by the Butler Center for Arkansas Studies, and asked me if I would be interested in writing the "foreword." He then informed me that Private Strong served in a Kansas Infantry Regiment on the western frontier. Because of my long-time interest in the Civil War on the border, dating to July 1956, when President Dwight D. Eisenhower signed into law legislation authorizing establishment of Pea Ridge National Military Park, this journal fired my interest.

I was not disappointed to read the manuscript and find that Strong and his regiment pulled most of their duty at Fort Smith in the District of the Frontier and in western Arkansas. The region and its people during the late 1950s to early mid-1960s were never far from my thoughts as I co-authored, with the much published western historian and late Arrell M. Gibson, *Fort Smith: Little Gibraltar on the Arkansas. Steele's Retreat from Camden and the Battle of Jenkins' Ferry* preceded this work in 1966. Experience gained in research for these books, as well as numerous monographs that appeared in the *Arkansas Historical Quarterly* during the years, disclosed that good Civil War soldiers' diaries and journals for this region are as scarce as hen's teeth.

A careful reading of *"A Rough Introduction to this Sunny Land": The Civil War Diary of Private Henry A. Strong, Co. K, Twelfth Kansas Infantry* as edited by Tom Wing was a rewarding experience. The observant Strong "tells it like it is" out on the western border. For soldiers and civilians it was a bitter conflict, far more so than east of the Mississippi Valley. Strong describes a war to the knife, and the knife to the hilt. Here, blacks, whites, and Indians in blue battled Confederates and their Indian allies. Hatreds, animosities and assassinations dating to "Bleeding Kansas" of the mid-1850s, when Freesoilers and Jayhawkers battled border ruffians and pro-slavery forces from Missouri, carried over into the Civil War. Bloody feuds were engendered that plagued the region long after Appomattox Court House.

Strong's jottings document that the farther west the war extended, the more savage it became. For people in the Shenandoah Valley the burning during "Red October" was a horrific experience, but few houses were torched and bushwhacking was not commonplace. The swath of destruction left by General William T. Sherman and his 60,000 soldiers and bummers on their "March to the Sea" and through the Carolinas saw no massacres or mass destruction of people's dwellings. The war was far different, however, on the western frontier. Destruction of homes and property was the norm. Brutal bushwhackings and murders were a way of life.

Tom Wing is a careful and thoughtful editor. He lets Private Strong tell his story absent the editor's heavy hand. The explanatory footnotes inform but do not overwhelm. Readers will find Strong and his comrades' war similar to the experiences of World War I doughboys and World War II G.I.s and Marines. There are long times between battles interrupted by days, weeks, and even months of marches, camps, boredom, "hurry up and wait" and homesickness.

Edwin C. Bearss
Historian Emeritus
National Park Service

Acknowledgements

Many people have encouraged me through the process of annotating this diary. I want to thank my wife and children for allowing me the time to complete this work and for the joy you bring to my life. I will always be indebted to Rosie Frey for bringing the diary to my attention. I wish to thank Ben Keppel for his guidance and direction. Julie Galonska deserves my thanks for her editorial suggestions and for helping me stay on track. I want to express my appreciation to Sue Schofield for her constant nudging, pushing and deadlines that helped me make it through the MLS program.

I am forever indebted to Edwin C. Bearss for his endorsement of the journal. Brian Robertson, Mark Christ, Frank Arey, and Billy Higgins have encouraged me throughout this process. Arnold Schofield provided important insight into the Kansas regiments and hours of stimulating conversation. Dr. Althea Rhodes has read my writing repeatedly to help it make sense.

I want to thank the descendents of Henry A. Strong: Charles Leamon, Carolyn Gleason, and Ralph Moody for allowing me to tell the story. It has been an honor to research this member of your family.

Lastly I am thankful to Henry A. Strong himself for taking the time to document his war experiences. At times, it appeared he did it just for me. His words have taught me so much about Fort Smith and Arkansas during the war and I have let them speak for themselves, only changing misspellings that made it difficult for the reader to understand.

Introduction

No other topic in American History is as popular as the Civil War. In the simplest terms the pro-slavery, southern, plantation agricultural states chose to secede from the United States and form a new country. While the war started over the right to leave the Union, many other issues fanned the flames of sectional conflict. Trade policies, for example, favored northeastern shipping interests and hindered the favorable trade relations between the South and the European nations. In addition, the expansion of slavery into new states coming into the Union inspired extensive bloodshed and fighting long before the firing on Fort Sumter in April of 1861. Arguments in the 1850s over whether the Kansas Territory would be a free or slave state came to a boiling point when anti-slavery forces clashed with pro-slavery advocates in western Missouri and eastern Kansas Territory. This prelude to the Civil War foreshadowed the bloody nature of the conflict to come.

Civil War historians have spent a great deal of time writing about the decisive battles and strategies of the war, yet a fair treatment of the fighting west of the Mississippi River is still missing. It seems ironic that the war is considered to be primarily a conflict between the North and South, yet academic study of the war, especially in recent years, has been more East and West in orientation. An examination of a typical academic press catalog will yield numerous titles relating to the Eastern Theater for every one relating to the conflict west of the Mississippi River. The war in the West has been largely forgotten. Yet incidents such as "Bleeding Kansas" and battles like Wilson's Creek (the second battle of the war) and Pea Ridge (a ray of hope for the Union in a year that produced some of its worst defeats) were highly significant. The first African-American regiment to see combat (First Kansas Colored Infantry) and the involvement of Native Americans on both sides are equally important. In addition, the only Native-American general and the last Confederate general to surrender (Stand Watie) is unknown to many Civil War scholars. Yet another forgotten detail is the sheer amount of destruction suffered in the areas of southwestern Missouri, southeastern Kansas, western

Arkansas, and Indian Territory.

The written sources on the Civil War in the West vary from detailed accounts of battles or campaigns to works that deal with the regional aspects. Only one book, Alvin Josephy's *The Civil War in the American West*, published in 1991, has attempted to illuminate all the fighting from the Mississippi River to the Pacific. Most other treatments of the West deal mainly with special topics such as individual Native-American tribes and their participation, African-American experiences, or regimental histories of units involved. The western Civil War has been the topic of many scholarly articles; some of the best are contained in the *Arkansas Historical Quarterly*, the *Journal of the West*, and the *Chronicles of Oklahoma*. The Civil War in the borderlands, more specifically southeast Kansas, southwest Missouri, western Arkansas, and Indian Territory has been treated a number of times over the years. In *Black Flag*, Thomas Goodrich discusses the guerilla warfare in Missouri and Kansas. *Rugged and Sublime*, edited by Mark Christ, is a detailed overview of the Civil War in Arkansas. Ed Bearss and A.M. Gibson's *Fort Smith: Little Gibraltar on the Arkansas* relates the role of Fort Smith, Arkansas, as a pre-war Federal outpost and Confederate staging and training area, and discusses its eventual reoccupation by Federal troops. Wiley Britton's *The Civil War on the Border* is a post-war memoir that discusses the main events of the border war from the perspective of a member of the Sixth Kansas Cavalry. Phillip Steele and Steve Cottrell's *Civil War in the Ozarks* is a light treatment of the destructive guerilla war and the pitched battles in southern Missouri and northwest Arkansas. *The American Indian as a Participant in the Civil War* by Annie H. Abel discusses Native-American participation within and outside of Indian Territory. G. W. Grayson's *A Creek Warrior for the Confederacy* discusses much of the action on the western border from the perspective of a Confederate Indian cavalryman. Kenny Franks outlines the involvement of the Cherokee and their greatest Confederate leader, Stand Watie, in *Stand Watie and the Agony of the Cherokee Nation*. *The Civil War in Indian Territory* by Larry Rampp and Donald Rampp is a complete treatment of the action in the Indian Nations. Still another complete treatment is Jay Monaghan's *The Civil War on the Western Border, 1854-1865*. Much of the fighting west of the Mississippi River involved horse soldiers; therefore Stephen Oates's *Confederate Cavalry West of the River* is an important contribution as well. Albert Castell's *A Frontier State at War: Kansas 1861-1865* and *Sterling Price and the Civil War in the West* give insight to these two important parts of the story. African-American troops played an important role in the action on the border. *The Sable Arm: Black Troops in the Union Army by* Dudley Taylor Cornish and Hondon Hargrove's *Black Union Soldiers in the Civil War* cover this very important aspect. Joseph Glatthaar takes a different approach in *Forged in Battle: The Civil War Alliance of Black Soldiers and White Officers.* In *Kansas in the Sixties*, Samuel Crawford discusses early action in Kansas and Missouri and later action in Indian Territory and Arkansas. John C. Waugh's *Sam Bell Maxey and the Confederate Indians* and Whit Edwards's *"The Prairie Was On Fire": First Hand Accounts of the Civil War in Indian Territory* focus almost completely on the action in Indian Territory.

In all the writing on the Civil War on the western border three common themes emerge: massive civilian suffering and destruction of property, lack of control in occupied areas by both sides, and wider participation among non-whites in the conflict. These themes show that the war in the West was just as significant to the lives of the people as the war was in the East. The typical soldier in the Western Theater suffered from the same difficulties the eastern soldier faced. Boredom, disease, homesickness, lack of pay and rations, and constant exposure to the elements were typical problems for soldiers everywhere. Yet the West differed from the East. At times the lines that divided the sides there were blurred and less distinct. A soldier on the western border was much more apt to become a victim of a bushwhacking by disguised troops than his eastern counterpart. But western soldiers also experienced fears and anxiety from large pitched battles and almost daily attrition from constant small-unit skirmishes and actions. All of these themes and experiences make up the story told in the diary of Private Henry A. Strong, Co. K, Twelfth Kansas Volunteer Infantry.

Henry Albert Strong was born in Stevenson County, Illinois, the second of six children. His parents were Lyman Strong and Hannah Montague. Strong's father was the postmaster at Mansfield, Kansas. At the time of enlistment, Henry was laboring as a farmer. He did not begin keeping a diary until fifteen months after he had entered service in the Twelfth Kansas Infantry. The first seven entries cover this fifteen-month period from August 1862 through October 1863. An examination of Strong's service records from the National Archives reveals that he joined the regiment on August 16, 1862, at Mound City, Kansas. All enlistment papers show Mound City as his place of residence. Mound City and surrounding Linn County were abolitionist strongholds in southeastern Kansas. Strong received a bounty of twenty-five dollars and a premium of two dollars for his three-year enlistment. His volunteer enlistment papers list him as five feet, ten inches tall with gray eyes, light hair, and fair complexion.

In the diary, Strong describes his experiences as a raw recruit and mentions the imported Austrian (Lorenz) muskets he was first issued before these were replaced with imported British (Enfield) muskets. Strong discusses his bout with the mumps and small pox and his regiment's near miss with Quantrill after the raid on Lawrence, Kansas. Beginning on October 1, 1863, Strong recorded daily entries, but these dwindled as the war claimed more of his time. From October to December 1863, the regiment was in southern Kansas and southwest Missouri. One important detail that Strong notes first here and continues to include throughout his writings is the daily number of miles marched, which is valuable in understanding the range and effectiveness of an infantry regiment. Another entry describes a letter Strong received from a friend and former member of Co. K., his "old mess mate" Montgomery. Only one Montgomery is found in the service records of the Twelfth Kansas: Charles J., son of James Montgomery, compatriot of John Brown and colonel of the Second South Carolina Colored Infantry.

At the end of October 1863, the Twelfth Kansas moved to Fort Scott. Many soldiers in the regiment acquired passes to go home. In December the regiment proceeded to Fort Smith, Arkansas. Strong was impressed with northeast Indian Territory and northwest Arkansas and described Fort Smith after arriving there December 28. The winter of 1863-64 was a particularly cold one by Arkansas standards, and Strong's misconceptions of the "sunny south" quickly gave way to an all-out effort to stay warm. From January through March of 1864, the Twelfth Kansas was on station at Fort Smith and periodically sent on escort and forage duty. In March, General Samuel Curtis, the commanding officer, ordered the city fortified with blockhouses, gun platforms, and rifle pits. The Twelfth Kansas participated in the construction of the fortifications. During the last few days of March 1864 all troops in Fort Smith prepared for an expedition south.

The Camden Expedition was part of a larger Red River Campaign that involved Federal efforts to occupy part of Texas. In a larger sense the campaign was also coordinated with Federal movements against Atlanta, Petersburg, Mobile, and the Shenandoah Valley. The Red River Campaign resulted in some of the most ferocious fighting in Arkansas during the war. In his notes on the action, Strong describes getting a "good long look" at the enemy for the first time. The campaign failed miserably at gaining a foothold in Texas. As a result, Federal control of Arkansas struggled for the next nine months. Strong and the Twelfth Kansas arrived back in Fort Smith by May 17. On June 15, Strong and twenty-four others from the Twelfth Kansas were detailed to protect a steamboat leaving Fort Smith for Fort Gibson, Indian Territory. Strong endured a harrowing adventure as the boat came under attack. Cherokee Confederate commander Stand Watie and his Indian troops later captured the boat and important stores of supplies.

In July and early August of 1864, Confederate forces, fresh from thwarting the Red River Campaign, spent six days probing the Federal position at Fort Smith. Strong describes the events of this action in fine detail including the execution of four bushwhackers and confirming the only time the garrison at Fort Smith ever came under attack in its lengthy history. In September, the regiment went to Fort Gibson in Indian Territory. Strong describes the Confederate "no quarter" policy as evidenced by a raid on a hay-cutting camp of the First Kansas Colored Infantry. In October, Strong observes with great interest Sterling Price's raid, which occurred near his hometown. After returning to Fort Smith, the regiment resumed escort and forage duty. Strong notes his one-year anniversary of arriving at Fort Smith in December. By February of 1865 the Twelfth Kansas was relocated to Little Rock. Strong notes the passing of major events throughout the winter and spring of 1865, most notably General Lee's surrender and the assassination of President Lincoln. On June 25, 1865, the Twelfth Kansas was relieved from duty and prepared to travel home. Strong's boat traveled down the White River to the Mississippi, then up to the Missouri River and across it to Wyandotte, where he received his discharge papers and turned in his equipment. Strong documented every town and steamboat passed on his journey. In 1867, he married Mary C. Madden and had one daughter, Loie. He owned and operated the H. A. Strong Mercantile Company in Mound City. In February of 1900, Strong acquired an invalid pension. He died in 1927 and his wife later received a widow pension.

Strong's diary exists in three forms: the original handwritten version, a transcription by the author's great granddaughter, and my transcription. I became acquainted with the diary in 1996 when Park Ranger Rosie Frey of Fort Scott National Historic Site sent a copy to Fort Smith National Historic Site. At the time, I was working as a seasonal ranger and researching the Civil War in Fort Smith. The diary helped to answer a number of questions concerning the Federal occupation of Fort Smith, and it documented a number of actions in the region. In 1998, I entered graduate school at the University of Oklahoma and became interested in the possibility of using the diary as a thesis project. I contacted Charles Leamon of Arma, Kansas, who donated the copy to Fort Scott. Mr. Leamon helped me contact Ralph Moody, a descendent of Private Strong, and he gave me permission to use it. After numerous readings, and while completing my own transcription, I annotated important events, people, and locations mentioned by Henry Strong.

The diary of Henry Strong is a rare look into the wartime life of an average Federal soldier in the West. His rank as a private sets the journal apart from officer's journals and diaries. While diaries of Eastern Theater soldiers are more common, few documents of this type exist. The reader will benefit from Strong's obvious possession of a quality education. For a young man barely out of his teens, he writes clearly and correctly. From a military history standpoint, the diary provides an invaluable picture into the lesser-understood actions in the "Border Region." Military historians will also be able to compare Strong's quality of soldier life with that of similar soldiers in the East. These aspects make the work relevant to the wide body of Civil War writing. However, the value of the document does not end with its military information. The diary shows in explicit detail three recurring themes mentioned earlier: civilian suffering and loss of property, uncertainty of control and authority, and wider participation among non-whites. Strong notes burned-out farms, deserted towns and constant foraging, all of which had drastic consequences for civilians. At times, Strong includes lines that describe a world of confusion and uncertainty. He illustrates this most with his recognition of the one-year anniversary of the Battle of Jenkins' Ferry and his surprise that things were so much better than they had been at the time of the battle. Finally, Strong constantly mentions the African- and Native-American troops he encountered. His writing is complimentary to the black troops's level of discipline and respectful towards the Confederate Indian troops's fighting ability. For these reasons and more, students, scholars, and the public should find the work a valuable resource.

Map showing some of the locations Strong visited during
his service in the Twelfth Kansas

Map by Mike Keckhaver

AUGUST 1862

Enlisted the United States Service August 16th, 1862, at Mound City, Kansas. Spent most of my time at home until September 10th, 1862. Then the company went into camp at Mound City and marched to Fort Lincoln on the Osage. Staid there over night. Several other companies had concentrated there from different parts of the state to organize a regiment.

SEPTEMBER

September 11th, Thursday
Started for Paola, Kansas. Camped at Mound City for the night. Next day marched to Twin Springs. This was Bully for greenhorns. We thought soldiering a fine thing. Would have enlisted for a lifetime, I presume, had any one proposed it. Arrived at Paola on the 12th, and at once went into a camp of instruction drilling from four to six hours per day in the strictest discipline. We were apt scholars, or most were, and made rapid progress in the art of soldiering. On 30th of September were mustered into U. S. Service for three years as the 12th Regiment-Kansas Vol. Infantry. Ours was Company "K", Capt. J. J. Sears, 1st Lt. P. J. Miserez, and 2nd Lt. Wm. Barrett. Spent the month of October in drawing arms, equipment and clothing, also drilling pretty regular. The guns were Austrian muskets and but of little account. The fore part of November marched back to Paola, camped on Bull Creek. Turned over the old muskets and drew Enfields Rifles, which are a splendid gun. From here marched out to Cold Water Grove, twenty miles east of Paola on the State Line. Were ordered to lay off a camp and fortify here. The boys

went on a forage trip over the line into Missouri in the night. Returned laden with chickens, mutton, and honey. Had jolly time. Staid there two nights and were ordered back to Paola. The latter part of November marched to Olathe. Col. Adams took one battalion of the Regt. and went into Missouri on an expedition – hardly know his object. Will not give my opinion here. Our company went with the Col., but I remained at Olathe quite unwell (with the mumps.) The expedition, or commander of it, got into innumerable difficulties. Was arrested and the command searched and sent back to Kansas. Our company remained at Olathe until the latter part of December, when the Capt. got permission to take the company to Mound City. Started and got as far as Paola where we were stopped by the Surgeon, as the small pox made its appearance in the company. Were sent to camp quarantine. Nearly all of the boys had the varioloid. I had a pretty hard siege of small pox. Was in the hospital from before Christmas until after New Years. So soon as I got able, got a leave of absence for five days and went home. [1]

---

[1] John J. Sears was from Mound City, Kansas, and was mustered in September 30, 1862. He was promoted major, Third Regiment Missouri Colored Volunteer Infantry, February 16, 1864. *Report of the Adjutant General of the State of Kansas, 1861-'65*, Vol. 1 (Topeka: Kansas State Print Co., 1896), 442.

Peter J. Miserez was from Mound City, Kansas, and was mustered in September 30, 1862. He was promoted captain in May of 1864, and mustered out with the regiment June 30, 1865. *Ibid.*

William Barrett was from Marmaton, Kansas, and was mustered in September 30, 1862, as second lieutenant. He was promoted first lieutenant May 26, 1864. He resigned May 20, 1865. *Ibid.*

Imported Austrian "Lorenz" muskets were widely distributed to infantry troops early in the war. With a tendency to collect fouling, they were usually replaced with more serviceable weapons at first opportunity. The British Pattern 1853 Enfield was widely used by both the North and the South, second only to the Springfield Model 1861. *Arms and Equipment of the Union* (Alexandria, VA: Time-Life Books, 1991), 36.

Charles W. Adams was from Lawrence, Kansas, and was mustered in September 30, 1862. He was wounded in action April 30, 1864, at Jenkins' Ferry, Arkansas. He was promoted brevet brigadier general February 13, 1865, and was mustered out with the regiment June 30, 1865. *Report of the Adjutant General*, 420.

Varioloid is a mild form of small pox.

1863

The first of February started to Fort Leavenworth. Were six days on the way. Had some of the coldest weather of the winter, and considerable snow to tramp through before getting there at night. Had to shovel away the snow to pitch our tents. Were put on post duty as soon as we arrived at the Fort. Had very good quarters in the barracks. Had to drill pretty regular, more style than necessary I thought. Had to wear white gloves at Dress Parades and Guard Mounting.

The latter part of April the company was ordered to Weston, Mo. (across the Missouri, six miles from the Fort) to quell a rebellion among the Militia. Staid there two days and returned to the Fort. Got several recruits while there. On the 3rd of May, our company was ordered to Kansas City, Missouri. Went on the Steamer "Majors". Tis thirty miles by water. Arrived at Kansas City and went on Provost duty. Capt. Sears commanding post. Had a splendid time while there. I had several adventures. Once on a trip across the river into Clay County, fell into the hands of the Paw Paw Militia. They talked of shooting me for being a Kansas Jayhawker. On the 4th of July, the Citizens presented the Company with a beautiful flag, worth one hundred and fifty dollars. It is the finest I ever saw. They also gave us a dinner. The flag made us feel pretty big. The latter part of June, General Ewing moved his Headquarters to this place, and the 11th Kansas Infantry came here, but were changed into a Cavalry Regt. The latter part of July our company got permission to go to Mound City and home. Staid there one month, was at home most of the time. Got quite a number of recruits for the Company at this time. It numbered one hundred and one men. Started back to Kansas

City the middle of August. Got there the 20th day. Lawrence was destroyed by Quantrill. Part of his command passed within a mile of our camp on Indian Creek east of Olathe in the night. I was taken sick and in the hospital two weeks with the fever just after we returned. We went out at the crossing of Blue and staid a week to protect the Stage between Kansas City and Independence from bushwhackers. The Company was then relieved by Cav. and returned to town. After that used to go across the Blue after apples, potatoes, chickens and lived splendid. Whenever we felt disposed, harnessed up the team and strike out to where twas plenty.[2]

About the 1st of October, Shelby and his command made their raid into Missouri, and we participated in the chase. From this on my diary is more exact. The account this far was taken up from memory, as the second is lost. From this on I will keep a daily diary.[3]

October 1st, Kansas City, Missouri
1st Thursday

On guard today at General Ewing's residence. Have taken Reynolds' place, he having gone home on furlough. I received a letter from Capt. Montgomery at Morris Island, South Carolina. He was my old mess-mate but was

---

[2] The fort Strong mentions is Fort Leavenworth, opposite Weston, Missouri, across the Missouri River.

The Paw Paw Militia was made up of pro-Southern men from western Missouri, conscripted into service for the federal government. During Price's Raid in 1864, many took the arms and equipment issued by federal authorities and joined Price's forces. The Paw Paw grows on a bush, and the fruit may appear on the outside to be ripe when in fact it is still unripe and sour. Pro-Southern conscripts were compared to the fruit because they appeared to be true blue on the outside, but had different feelings hidden inside. Kip Lindberg, telephone interview with editor, 2001.

William Clarke Quantrill was a native of Ohio and became a noted outlaw in Kansas before the Civil War under the alias "Charley Hart." Officially commissioned a captain in the Confederate Army, Quantrill was associated with "Bloody Bill" Anderson, the Youngers, and the James brothers and developed a reputation for ruthless guerrilla tactics. Best known for his raid on Lawrence, Kansas, in August of 1863, he went to Kentucky in 1864 and was shot and captured. He died June 6, 1864. Albert E. Castel, *William Clarke Quantrill: His Life and Times* (Norman: University of Oklahoma Press, 1999).

[3] Joseph O. Shelby was born in Kentucky but moved to Missouri and had a prosperous

promoted to Capt. in a colored Regt. in South Carolina and left the company in August.[4]

October 2nd, Friday

I am on camp guard today and night. One of the recruits, Leahy, deserted. He tried to rob the Paymaster, was detected and left. A number of us went across Blue today, took a Govt. wagon and loaded it with apples, potatoes, chickens, turkeys & etc. Everything good almost. Got a large supply of forages.[5]

---

hemp plantation before the war. A slave owner and pro-slavery advocate, he became involved in the border war prior to the Civil War. He organized and financed a cavalry company and joined Sterling Price's forces. He fought at Wilson's Creek, Pea Ridge, and Prairie Grove and also against Steele's Red River Campaign. He was promoted brigadier general in December of 1862. He refused to surrender in 1865 and fled with many followers to Mexico but came back to Missouri in 1867. He was appointed U.S. Marshal for the Western District of Missouri in 1893. He died in 1897. William L. Shea, *War in the West: Pea Ridge and Prairie Grove* (Abilene, TX: McWhiney Foundation Press, 1998), 89.

[4] Thomas Ewing was brother-in-law to William T. Sherman, and had two brothers (Hugh and Charles) who were also Union generals. Thomas Ewing was colonel of the Eleventh Kansas Cavalry and served in various administrative posts on the frontier. In 1863 he was assigned to the border region of western Missouri and issued his infamous "Order #11," which depopulated four Missouri counties to curb guerilla activity. He was later transferred to St. Louis and helped counter Price's raid in 1864. He resigned in 1865 and served two terms in Congress as a Democrat after the war. Stewart Sifakis, *Who Was Who in the Union: A Comprehensive, Illustrated Biographical Reference to More Than 1,500 of the Principal Union Participants in the Civil War* (New York: Facts on File, 1988), 130.

Hiram Reynolds was from Mound City, Kansas. He enlisted August 2, 1863, and mustered out in Little Rock, Arkansas, June 30, 1865. *Report of the Adjutant General*, 444.

Charles J. Montgomery enlisted September 10, 1862, and was promoted corporal September 30, 1862. On July 1, 1863, he was promoted captain and transferred to the Second South Carolina Colored Infantry. His father, James Montgomery, was a devoted abolitionist and associate of John Brown. James was also colonel of the Second South Carolina Colored Infantry. Charles is listed as Charles S. in the Kansas Adjutant General's Report, but is listed as Charles J. on the Twelfth Kansas enlistment roll on file at the Kansas State Historical Society. *Ibid.*, 442.

[5] Thomas Leahy enlisted September 1, 1863, and deserted September 28, 1863, near

October 3, Saturday
Nothing of interest occurred today. Very cool and windy. Quite winter like.

October 4, Sunday
I'm on guard again today. Very windy and dusty.

October 5, Monday
Orderly Cook started to Illinois this morning on furlough.[6]

October 6th, Tuesday
Peter Eby started home this morning. Why am not I lucky or smart enough to get a furlough. Went to party at Mrs. Lobodie's. Had a splendid time, dancing and a supper also. Received a letter from home. Weather very pleasant.[7]

October 7th, Wednesday
Cold and dreary weather. Wrote a letter to Mother. Were ordered to be ready to march at ten o'clock with six days' rations. The hours at length rolled round and we were put into wagons at the rate of twelve to a wagon. The command consisted of a Battalion of the 10th and 12th Infantry under command of Gen. Ewing and started out into Missouri, not knowing our destination. Were after Rebels and would go where they were. Passed through Westport, then on to Hickman's Mill. Passed just before sundown and went on to Pleasant Hill. Arrived there at midnight and went into camp. Distance 35 miles today.

October 8th, Thursday
Broke camp at 8 o'clock this morning. By this time the command that had concentrated here numbered upward of fifteen hundred. Marched south today. Arrived at Harrisonville by sunset. Stopped long enough to get supper. Then traveled to a little deserted town called Austin, ten miles from Harrisonville.

Kansas City. *Ibid.,* 444.

[6] Horace B. Cook was from Linn County, Kansas. He enlisted August 16, 1862, and was promoted first sergeant September 30, 1862. He was promoted second lieutenant on May 26, 1864. *Ibid.,* 442.

[7] Peter Eby was from Marmaton, Kansas, and enlisted September 3, 1862. *Ibid.,* 443.

Very difficult getting along as the night was very dark. Distance today – thirty miles.

October 9th, Friday
Started this morning just after sunrise and went to within ten miles of Butler. The Gen. received a dispatch that the enemy were making toward Booneville east of us. Here we took a northeast course striking across prairies or through the timber without any road. Had to pick a road for the wagons. Camped at dusk at Grand River for the night. Fired a grist mill near camp. I am on camp guard tonight. Distance today – twenty miles.

October 10th, Saturday
Broke up camp early this morning and marched to within ten miles of Warrensburgh and camped. I was out with the forage train. Got lots of honey and chickens and plenty of apples. Capt. Sears came up to command tonight from Kansas City. Had the hardest kind of a rain. Commenced just before we got supper cooked and we were to go without, with the exception of a little "hard tack", but did not relish that much as we were used to chicken, honey and other good things. Traveled twenty-five miles.

October 11th, Sunday
Marched to Warrensburgh and camped for dinner. Wrote a letter to Libby. The people welcomed us to town with flags and banners flying....quite an excitement. After dinner marched through the whole long of the town. The ladies gave the boys quite a number of the Starry Banners. We had one and some two or three flags to the wagon. On the whole twas quite an exciting time. We got to Knob Noster at eight p.m. Went into camp. Has the appearance of rain. Last night we got a good wetting under the Government wagons – was all the shelter we had, and they were not sufficient for half of the command. Distance – thirty miles, today.[8]

October 12th, Monday
We started early this morning and marched to within two miles of Sedalia and camped waiting for the scouts of report. About three o'clock, the Gen. received information that the rebels were marching on Booneville. It commenced to rain and rained so hard that we did not get started until dusk.

---

[8] Libby was Strong's sister.

Passed through Sedalia and Georgetown, and went toward Booneville. The night was very dark and raining all the time. Made it difficult to get along at all. Had to build fires along the road to light up the way, so we could see to get over rough places. Dragged along until two o'clock in the morning, when the artillery got so stuck fast in the mud that it was impossible to extricate it until daylight. A number of the wagons were overturned, and we had either to walk through the mud or run the risk of getting crippled. Two or three were severely injured by the upsetting of the wagon they were in. Distance during the day and night – 25 miles.

October 13th, Tuesday
Learning that the Rebels had turned up the river from Booneville, we turned and marched northwest from Booneville. Passed through a very rough and hilly country, where there was an abundance of persimmons, which we more than "went for". Got to camp a little after dark. Very tired and sleepy. Distance only twelve miles.

October 14th, Wednesday
Marched into Knob Noster. Could hear nothing of the enemy. At one o'clock a scout of Cavalrymen dashed into town and reported the Rebels close on us. Part of the scouts were captured only eight miles northeast of town an hour before. We turned back two miles and camped on a small creek to await what the next few hours would develop. Yesterday Gen. Brown's forces had a fight with the Rebels at Marshal, twenty miles distant resulting in Brown's capturing two pieces of artillery and quite a number of prisoners. Traveled 18 miles. [9]

October 15th, Thursday
Received notice at midnight that the enemy were marching south as fast as they could go and only six miles west of us. Were roused up as quickly as possible and started at one o'clock. Passed through Knob Noster and Warrensburgh. Got to the latter place at daylight. Took a southern course.

---

[9] E.B. Brown was a former mayor of Toledo, Ohio. He moved to Missouri and held various positions with the state militia and federal volunteers. He was wounded in 1863, and during Price's raid in 1864 he was arrested for disobeying General Pleasonton's orders. The charges were later dropped. He resigned November 10, 1865, and worked as a pension agent and farmer after the war. Sifakis, *Who Was Who in the Union*, 48.

Struck the trail of Rebels six miles from Warrensburgh, two hours after the main command had passed. The rear guard was still in sight. Now the chase commenced in earnest. We have had no breakfast, but there is no stopping now. We got out of the wagons at the crossing of the Grand River and double quicked six miles then formed into a line supposing that we were pretty near the Rebels. The Col. made a few remarks and then we started on again fast as we could go. Saw several horses that were tired out and turned loose by the Rebels. Stopped just before sundown having marched fifteen miles since leaving the wagons, to rest and wait for the wagons to come up. We looked around to find something to eat. Found some potatoes buried and killed a hog and roasted them. Made a dinner out of it. At eight o'clock the wagons came up. We traveled two hours longer and camped for the night in woods where Major Ransom's Cavalry came up with the rear guard of the Rebels and had a skirmish. Killed two of them and took some prisoners. Distance since one o'clock this morning 65 miles. Had only one meal today and that consisted of pork and potatoes roasted over the fire.[10]

October 16th, Friday
Started at daylight this morning. Traveled to the Osage River and camped for dinner. While a detail was sent to the river bottom to cut a road through for wagons and artillery. The Rebs have no artillery or train now. Their whole command is on horseback, and they are not particular whether they keep the road or not their object is to make all the speed possible and take a course that will bother us the most. We have passed several places where the Rebels have stopped and hastily prepared a meal of victuals and fed their horses from some cornfield. Crossed the Osage River at sundown. Had to let the wagons and artillery down the bank of the river. After getting out of the river bottom, came onto a beautiful prairie, over which we traveled very rapidly till ten o'clock at night, when we came into the timbers and lost our way. An alarm was raised, and we all got out in line in the brush and staid an hour, but it proved a false alarm, and so we laid down in the grass and slept till morning as all were very tired. Distance – 36 miles.

October 17, Saturday
Col. Weer with eight hundred Cavalry came up last night. Started on this

---

[10] Wyllis C. Ransom was from Fort Scott, Kansas, and enlisted March 14, 1862. He mustered out March 18, 1865, at Devalls Bluff, Arkansas. *Report of the Adjutant General*, 164.

morning traveling south. Stopped at noon to feed the teams and left them. It is a very windy day and the fire got out in the grass. Could not put it out.

Burned one wagon, some mules and a few other articles. Kept on and in the night were joined by the 9th Kansas and the Kansas Militia. Crossed the Ozark Mountains and more prairie, over which we traveled very rapidly. The mountains consisted of rolling ridges, ridge after ridge until we reached the summit. Then it descended the same way. The prairie was all on fire, which was a grand scene. We're so close on the Rebs that a bridge across the North Fork of Spring River near Lamar, that they fired after crossing was not yet burned down. This delayed us some but we went up the stream two miles and crossed. Struck into the road again and kept on all night. Was awful sleepy. There were so many in the wagon that we could not lie down any. The Rebs thinking that they were safe had camped near Carthage. Stopped within one mile of that place at daylight. Distance in the twenty four hours – 50 miles.[11]

October 18, Sunday
We formed (left the wagon) and waded Spring River and charged into Carthage just at sunrise. Captured 28 prisoners there. They hastily left their camp before we could come on to them. Our teams were tired out and we gave up the chase. Camped at Carthage for the day. First day of rest since we started out.

October 19, Monday
Moved six miles southeast of town on a small stream. Camped by a large orchard where there is plenty of apples. Was over part of the battlefield of Sigel.[12]

October 20, Tuesday
Moved camp on Jones Creek two miles west. Plenty of honey, chickens and etc. Are getting pretty well rested.

---

[11] William Weer was commissioned colonel of the Tenth Kansas Cavalry June 20, 1861. He was dismissed from service by General Order No. 123 August 20, 1864. He was dishonorably discharged, but it was reversed in 1865. *Report of the Adjutant General*, 347.

[12] The "Battlefield of Sigel" is Carthage, Missouri, where Colonel Franz Sigel tangled with Governor Claiborne Jackson's pro-secession forces in June of 1861.

October 21, Wednesday

The Militia and all the wagons started for Fort Scott and left us to take in on foot, soldier fashion. The prisoners taken at Carthage went out to Fort Scott with the exception of four that enlisted in Company G of our Regt. The command started at two o'clock and marched South to Shoal Creek, fifteen miles. Did not make camp till late at night.

October 22, Thursday

Rained and snowed last night. So we got very wet. Rained all the morning. Shoal Creek pretty deep. Had to wade it. Twas a pretty cold bath. Marched into Neosho, three miles from the creek and went into houses to out of the storm. Snowed all day. Was four or five inches deep. Two of the captured Rebels that enlisted in Co. G were recognized by Missouri Militia as a Bushwhacker and the General turned them over to the Militia, who immediately shot them. Their bodies were left lying out in the street all that day and night.

October 23rd, Friday

Started early this morning and marched east. Very cold. Camped by a large spring, quite a curiosity – the largest spring I ever saw. There is a saw mill only a short distance below the spring. It furnishes sufficient water to run the mill. There is an abundance of apples and potatoes in the house we camped by, which we helped ourselves to. 15 miles today.

October 24th, Saturday

Marched ten miles today and camped at Rocky Comfort (a very peculiar name by the way), although suiting the place with one exception, very well as the rocks were the predominant, but could not see the comfort part of it. The snow has all disappeared. We'll start for Fort Scott in the morning. All are jubilant. We are needing some more clothes badly.

October 25th, Sunday

Started early this morning and went toward Kansas. Passed through Newtonia and camped at Granby. At Newtonia the boys could get some tobacco. They were all out of the luxury and nearly crazy for it. As soon as they got into town they more than went for it. At Granby are lead mines. Distance today – 22 miles.

October 26th, Monday

Marched to Carthage. Camped on Spring River. Done some good marching.

Are going toward home now. Distance – 25 miles.

October 27th, Tuesday
Ran a race with the 10th Kansas today. We camped for the night five miles ahead of them. Passed through Lamar and camped on the north fork of the Spring River. 27 miles.

October 28th, Wednesday
Started a long time before daylight and marched to Ft. Scott. Got there at ten in the night. Crossed the Ozark prairie. Met a large train and a Battalion of our Regt. And the 2nd Kansas Colored on their way to Fort Smith, Arkansas. Passed them on Dry Wood. The 10th Kansas could not catch up with us. We outran them on the march. Commenced to rain in the afternoon and rained all that night. Twas pretty muddy before we got to the Fort. Distance 35 miles.

October 29th Thursday
Rained hard all day. Drew clothing and rations and part of us started afternoon for Mound City. Had ten leaves of absence for the company to go home. We got as far as Fort Lincoln by dark, wet as water could make us. Put up at a house. Got partly dry by the fire. Slept on the floor, which we did not grumble at. We were tired out. 12 miles.

October 30th, Friday
Snowed last night so twas awful cold this morning. Started at daylight and got to Mound City at eight o'clock and then went home. There was a man hung at the Mound today, named Griffin. Was glad to get home once more. Staid there and through the neighborhood until November eight, when the Company met at Mound City to march North.[13]

November 8th, Sunday
Staid at home till today. Co. met at Mound City and started at sunrise for Osawatomie. Marched fifteen miles and camped on Middle Creek. Very

---

[13]William Griffith was one of the perpetrators of the Marais des Cygnes Massacre in 1858. Five men were killed and five wounded by pro-slavery raiders near the community of Trading Post, Kansas. Griffith was caught and sentenced to hang at Mound City, October 23, 1863. Doris Purvis, *A Little History About Mound City, Kansas* (Mound City, KS: Mound City Historical Society, 1976), 20.

cold night.

November 9th, Monday
Marched into Osawatomie – ten miles – early this morning. The whole Co. met here today. Lt. Barrett and the boys from Kansas City arrived also with all of our baggage. Went into camp on the north side of the North Fork of the Marais Des Cygnes. Staid here until the 22nd of the month. Spent our time in hunting and fishing. Not much duty to do only camp ground to keep up – have a fine time in and around town.

November 22nd, Sunday
Paymaster arrived but would not pay us off as no Commissioned Officers was present. We all started for home then or all that wanted to. Got home that night. Twenty five miles.

November 23rd, Monday
At home. Today are to go on to Fort Scott as soon as the company comes by.

November 24th, Tuesday
The company came by and camped at Mound City tonight. I staid home.

November 25th, Wednesday
I joined the company early this morning, and we marched to Fish Creek. Fifteen miles.

November 26th, Thursday
Got into Fort Scott at noon – went into camp on the Marmaton above town. Were paid off this afternoon. Remained at Scott until the 13th of December, preparing to go south – no duty to do scarcely. Had battalion drill nearly every day – quite an easy time. Some very cold weather.

December 13th, Sunday
Started for Fort Smith, Arkansas this morning. Cold and rainy day. Marched twelve miles to Drywood, and camped for the night. The Command consisted of six companies of the 12th Kansas and some Cavalry, train of two hundred Government wagons and one hundred Sutler wagons. Very cold camping out. Twelve miles.

December 14th, Monday
Marched ten miles and camped on Little Drywood. Still very cold.

December 15th, Tuesday
Started early this morning and marched all day. Twenty three miles. Camped on North Fork of Spring River. Commenced to snow before we got our tents pitched and snowed all the evening. Crossed the Ozark prairie, twenty miles across it.

December 16th, Wednesday
Marched 13 miles to Spring River and camped for the night. It rained and sleeted all day, so we got very wet. Twas an awful cold day. Very disagreeable marching. Had to wade Spring River and several other small streams.

December 17th, Thursday
Awful cold this morning. If was colder when we left Scott, tis "colder" now. Snow several inches deep and still snowing. Marched ten miles to Turkey Creek Lead mines and camped for the train to come up. Some of the Sutler wagons have broken down. Passed through the town of Sherwood, which was burned by the Rebels one year and a half ago. Come across a fine lot of hogs which we more than went for, being the first we have come across.

December 18th, Friday
Laid by today for the wagons that are broken down to be repaired. Went out in the country five miles to get some apples. Saw the first family since leaving Drywood. We are camped six miles east of Baxter Springs where Gen. Blunt's band was murdered two or three months since. Weather moderating.[14]

---

[14] James Gilpatrick Blunt was born in Maine but moved to Kansas and was a physician by trade. He was involved in the anti-slavery movement before the war. He was commissioned brigadier general April 8, 1862, and promoted to major general November 29, 1862. Blunt led troops at Cane Hill and Prairie Grove in Arkansas, and Honey Springs in Indian Territory. He had a reputation as a fighter but did not get along well with the high command. On October 6, 1863, General Blunt and a small escort including his band were traveling to Fort Smith, Arkansas, and passed through Baxter Springs, Kansas. Approaching the town, Blunt saw blue uniformed horsemen and assumed the garrison was greeting him. The horsemen turned out to be Quantrill and his men who had Blunt significantly outnumbered. Blunt barely escaped with his life. Many

December 19th, Saturday

Marched eighteen miles and camped on Lost Creek tonight. Crossed Shoal Creek on the ice. Passed the town of Grand Falls. Went to the falls. They are quite a curiosity. It makes a splendid mill since there is a natural dam there. Saw some splendid country prairie and timber. After crossing Shoal Creek tis hilly and all timbered land. Eighteen miles.

December 20th, Sunday

Marched twenty two miles and camped at the General Mills on Elk Creek. These mills are the ones that furnished Price's Army with flour, while camped on Cowskin Prairie. His famous camp of instruction in 1861. Seven Sutler wagons broke down today. Very rough road crossed small streams.[15]

December 21st, Monday

Marched sixteen miles and camped at Maysville, Arkansas.   Crossed Cowskin Prairie. Struck the northwest corner of Arkansas at ten o'clock. Gave three cheers of Rackensack. Beautiful country around Maysville Prairie. Interspersed with timber. Got two wagon loads of apples at a Rebel's and divided out to Regt. All in gay spirits.[16]

December 22nd, Tuesday

A member of Co. "I" died last night. Was buried this morning under a clump of trees southwest of town with military honors far away from home and the dearest friends on earth. After paying the last sad tribute to our deceased

---

of his escort and band were not so fortunate. Jay Monaghan, *Civil War on the Western Border* (Boston: Little, Brown, 1955), 293.

[15] Sterling Price was born in Virginia but moved to Missouri in 1831. He practiced law and served in the legislature. He was colonel of the Second Missouri Infantry in the Mexican War. He was promoted brigadier general and appointed military governor of New Mexico. He was governor of Missouri from 1853 to 1857. He was opposed to secession but also opposed extreme unionism. He led troops at Wilson's Creek, Pea Ridge, Iuka, Corinth, Helena, and Steele's Camden Expedition. In 1864 he led a raid into Missouri and Kansas. He went to Mexico after the war but returned to Missouri in 1866. He died in St. Louis September 29, 1867. Stewart Sifakis, *Who Was Who in the Confederacy: A Comprehensive, Illustrated Biographical Reference to More Than 1,000 of the Principal Confederacy Participants in the Civil War* (New York: Facts on File, 1988), 231.

[16] Rackensack was a nickname for Arkansas.

comrade, we marched thirteen miles and camped near the west line of Arkansas. Crossed Spavenaugh Creek and mountains, a spur of the Bostons which are in sight. Saw some pine for the first time. The advance ran on to some of Stan Waite's men just before we got to camp this evening. Killed three and took four prisoners. Stan Waite's force supposed to be two hundred and fifty. Weather warm and pleasant. Mud drying up quite fast – easier marching.[17]

December 23rd, Wednesday
Marched twenty miles today and camped at Cincinatti, a little town near the line, but tis nearly deserted. Crossed Illinois River, had to wade it. Twas very cold. This is the largest stream we have crossed on the trip. Tis a very hilly country, getting on toward the Boston Mountains.

December 24th, Thursday
Laid over at Cincinatti today. "Our Mess" went out into the country after some eatables. Got plenty of apples and fresh pork. Saw lots of pretty girls, but all pretty strong Rebels. Cloudy with the appearance of rain.

December 25th, Friday
Christmas. We marched eighteen miles and camped on a small creek in the Cherokee Nation. Passed Cane Hill to the left. Mountainous country still. Commenced raining as we got to camp and rained all night.

---

[17] Stand Watie was born in Georgia and was three-quarter Cherokee. He signed the removal treaty with Major Ridge and Elias Boudinot. Ridge and Boudinot were killed for their role in the treaty negotiations. Watie survived an attempt on his life. Watie was a slave owner and had a thriving plantation in Indian Territory when the war broke out. Watie offered his services to the Confederacy when the Cherokee Nation split along old tribal factions over support for the war. Watie's men took part in Pea Ridge and many smaller actions in the border region where he attained a reputation as a brilliant cavalry commander. He was the only Native American to achieve the rank of general during the war and the last Confederate general to surrender. He died in 1871 while trying to recoup his lost fortune. Kenny A. Franks, *Stand Watie and the Agony of the Cherokee Nation* (Memphis: Memphis State University Press, 1979).

Thomas Martin was from Lanesfield, Kansas, and enlisted August 21, 1862. He died of disease at Maysville, Arkansas, December 22, 1863. *Report of the Adjutant General*, 439.

December 26th, Saturday

Marched seventeen miles and camped on Cove Creek. Crossed it thirteen times during the day. Wet and rainy all day.

December 27th, Sunday

Marched twelve miles and camped on the side of a mountain as the teams could not get over it. It was so wet and slippery.

December 28th, Monday

Started early this morning. Are out of rations, too. Got to Fort Smith at one o'clock. Twelve miles today. Crossed the Arkansas River in wagons. Went into camp with the rest of Regt. that was here. Fort Smith is a very pretty place, or was before the war. There are several churches in the place. Shade trees along the streets, besides barracks are buildings in the garrison. There are a great number of Government buildings.

December 29th, Tuesday

Spent the day in looking around town and writing home. Am glad that we are at our journey's end for the present, as I am pretty well tired out.

December 30th, Wednesday

Rained nearly all day. Sent to Van Buren after rations. There seems to be a scarcity of grub here. At least we can't get it.

December 31st, Thursday

Snowed all last night. Six inches deep this morning. Mustered for pay today.

The Thirteenth Kansas Infantry in formation on Garrison Avenue in Fort Smith, November 12, 1864.

Photographs courtesy of
Jules Martino

1864

January 1st, Friday
Very cold weather, I think, for the "sunny South". Snow six inches deep. Had nothing for breakfast this morn except what we could buy. Rather a rough introduction to this "Sunny land".

January 2nd, Saturday
Started on foraging trip out in the country, Fifty of Co. "K" under Lt. Barrett with ten wagons. Traveled east to Greenwood, eighteen miles. Got lost and did not get to the town until ten o'clock that night. Very cold now lying on the ground.

January 3rd, Sunday
Traveled eighteen miles and camped at dark at Mr. Cotner's away in the mountains somewhere. Tis cloudy and I am completely lost, don't know which way north is even. We are in Scott County, I am told. Are to load the wagons at this place with corn. Mr. Cotner let some sleep in his house –all that could get in. The rest staid in the barn.

January 4th, Monday
Loaded the train with corn and started on the return. Traveled seven miles and camped at Garrison's Mills in between the hills. Are in Franklin County. Snowed nearly all day. Is getting pretty deep.

January 5th, Tuesday
We marched ten miles from Fort Smith. We camped on Big Creek eighteen

miles from Fort Smith. We staid at Cpt. Brooks' house. This is the coldest day of the season. We passed by a peculiar mound today called Potatoe Hill. It is right in the prairie and has pine trees on it. Tis very high.[18]

January 6th, Wednesday
Marched eighteen miles and got to Ft. Smith at two o'clock. Found all the boys alive trying to keep from freezing. They suffer more from the cold in camp than we did while out. I must confess that this is rather disagreeable soldiering.

January 7th, Thursday
Co. "D" started on a foraging trip today. Snowing more today. The temperature more suitable for Wisconsin than this latitude.

January 8th, Friday
Cloudy and as cold as ever. Spent the day in camp. Tried to keep warm by taking a kettle of coals into my tent. Answered very well until they died out, and cook objected to my taking any more for the fire.

January 9th, Saturday
Cleared off today. Thawed some. Co. "C" returned from a foraging trip. Hardly know what to do am so lonesome. Want to hear from home.

January 10th, Sunday
On guard today in the Garrison. General Inspection. Our company gets the praise of being the finest company in the Regt. I guarded the Rebel prisoners. Had a long talk with some of them. Some are willing to give up the Confederacy, while others have great confidence in this Confederacy.

January 11, Monday
An escort started to Fort Scott. Sent two letters by them. The Arkansas River is all frozen over so that teams cross on the ice. The citizens say that is the coldest winter that has been known for twenty years. Weather moderated down to within the bounds of reason again.

---

[18] Potato Hill is about twenty miles from Fort Smith near Charleston, Arkansas. Since 1941, it has been in the impact area of the Fort Chaffee Military Reservation.

January 12, Tuesday
Nothing new today. Everything jogs along as usual. John Dunbar commenced to cook for Mess No. 2, as Jim Tyhurst has opened the Post bakery.[19]

January 13, Wednesday
Cloudy with the appearance of rain. Attended church this evening. Heard a very able sermon on the Creation of the World.

January 14, Thursday
Had squad drill this morning. The boys grumbled considerable. Think that we are too old soldiers to drill any more. Ball playing is got to be a chief amusement. Well, anything to drive away the Blues when a fellow is on short rations.

January 15th, Friday
A large train arrived from Little Rock. Prospect of an increase of grub. We are really in need of this, as had nothing for breakfast.

January 16th, Saturday
Thirty three of Co. "K" (myself included) and thirty of Co. "F" under command of Lt. Town of Co. "B", started on a foraging trip out in the country. Camped three miles out from Fort Smith. Train consists of one hundred wagons.[20]

January 17, Sunday
Traveled seventeen miles and camped on Big Creek. We ride whenever we choose to. Some of the boys eat in the wagons and played cards all day.

January 18th, Monday
Got to Roseville tonight –distance twenty three miles. Passed through the little town of Charleston. One train and part of Co. "K" loaded near here

---

[19]John Dunbar was from Mound City, Kansas, enlisted August 29, 1862, and was discharged with the regiment June 30, 1865. *Report of the Adjutant General*, 443.

James Tyhurst was from Mound City, Kansas, and enlisted August 16, 1862. He mustered out with the regiment June 30, 1865. *Ibid.*, 444.

[20]Martin L. Town was from Lawrence, Kansas, and was commissioned second lieutenant August 15, 1862. He was promoted first lieutenant March 6, 1865. He was mustered out with the regiment June 30, 1865. *Ibid.*, 425.

and started back to Smith. Roseville is on the Arkansas River over forty miles below Fort Smith. The 1ˢᵗ Kansas Colored Regt. are stationed here under Col. Williams. They are gathering in cotton and corn for the Government.[21]

January 19ᵗʰ, Tuesday

Weather clear and pleasant. Went down the river two miles on a large plantation where there was over one thousand acres in corn, and gather it out of the field. Got all of the wagons loaded by noon. There are large plantations of corn and cotton, which the planters had their slaves put in and tend until July or August, when the Federals took Fort Smith. They took their darkies and went farther south, where they were safer and left their crops unharvested. There is also an abundance of fat hogs running loose that we more than "go for".

January 20ᵗʰ, Wednesday

Traveled eighteen miles and camped one mile west of Charleston. Made the hogs suffer that crossed our path. Are taking several into camp. I am on guard tonight.

January 21ˢᵗ, Thursday

Arrived at Ft. Smith at 4 p.m. Quite a pleasant trip on the whole. Cos. "C" and "G" have gone to Little Rock with Rebel prisoners.

January 22ⁿᵈ, Friday

Very warm and pleasant. Had Battalion drill this afternoon. WM. Ingram and Howard released from the guardhouse where they have been for twenty-three days under false charges.[22]

---

[21] James M. Williams was commissioned captain in the Fifth Kansas Cavalry on July 12, 1861. He was promoted colonel and transferred to the First Kansas Colored Infantry May 2, 1863. He was promoted brevet brigadier general February 13, 1865, and was discharged October 1, 1865. *Report of the Adjutant General*, 574.

[22] William D. Ingrum was from Mound City, Kansas, and joined the regiment August 5, 1863. He mustered out with the regiment June 30, 1865. *Ibid.*, 444.

William A. Howard joined the regiment April 26, 1863, and was mustered out June 30, 1865. *Ibid.*

January 23rd, Saturday

Weather warm and pleasant. Regimental train returned from foraging. The only way we can get grub enough is to send out from Regt. independent of what we get from the Commissary Department. Am tired of doing nothing. When every other reason has failed I fall back on the old, old game of uchre.[23]

January 24th, Sunday

On guard in the Garrison at Post No. 1 at the gate. While on the post, thought of friends far away, yes, far away.

January 25th, Monday

Got a pass and went to town and looked around a little. A forage train attacked by bushwhackers near Charleston. One teamster killed and four wounded. The escort formed and drove them off. Had drill again.

January 26th, Tuesday

Mail came in last night. Got two letters, the first since leaving Fort Scott. There wasn't a more pleased fellow than myself just at that time.

January 27th, Wednesday

Very warm and pleasant. Springlike. Col. Steele got back from his scout toward Red River. Brought one whole company of Rebel prisoners, taken below Sugar Loaf Mountain.[24]

January 28th, Thursday

Train from Fort Scott arrived tonight. Capt. Bunn came with it. He brought me a letter from Sister Libbie. The contents of which I quickly perused. One month today since we arrived at Ft. Smith.[25]

---

[23] Uchre was a popular card game played by the soldiers in camp. Many references to this game are found in other diaries and journals of Civil War soldiers.

[24] James M. Steele was from Lawrence, Kansas, and was commissioned captain, Co. E, Twelfth Kansas Infantry on September 26, 1862. He was promoted lieutenant colonel, 113th United States Colored Infantry, January 16, 1864. *Report of the Adjutant General*, 10.

[25] Ezekiel Bunn was from Mansfield, Kansas, and was commissioned captain September 30, 1862. He resigned February 10, 1865, at Little Rock, Arkansas. *Ibid.*, 434.

January 29th, Friday

Am on picket guard on the Little Rock road. A storm came up in the afternoon. I happened to be in camp. The water ran all through my tent and was about to wash everything away. My tent was blown over and left me out in the "wet". Everything got as wet as water could make it. Cos. "A" and "I" moved over into the Garrison. Received a letter from home.

January 30th, Saturday

Weather cleared up and warm again. Wrote a letter to Libbie. Nothing occurred today to raise any excitement.

January 31st, Sunday

Another storm of wind and rain. My tent blew over again and got a worse wetting than before. But I was not alone this time. Half of the tents in the Regt. blew down. Had Inspection this morning. Attended church. Subject Lazarus and the Rich Man.

February 1st, Monday

A change in our mess affairs. Carpenter takes Dunbar's place as cook. The Regt. are raising a subscription to buy Col. Hayes a sword and revolvers to cost twelve hundred dollars. Gen. Thayer, the new commander arrived and assumed command of Division.[26]

February 2nd, Tuesday

On guard today at the Garrison. Rations played out. Had no supper.

---

[26] Chester B. Carpenter was from Mound City, Kansas, and joined the regiment August 16, 1862. He died from fever in Fort Smith, October 25, 1864. *Report of the Adjutant General*, 443.

Josiah E. Hayes was from Olathe, Kansas, and was commissioned lieutenant colonel September 30, 1862. He was promoted brevet brigadier general and was wounded as well as captured at Jenkins' Ferry, Arkansas, April 30, 1864. He was exchanged February 25, 1865, and mustered out July 15, 1865. *Ibid.*, 420.

John M. Thayer was a native of Massachusetts. He moved to Nebraska Territory before the war. He fought at Fort Donelson, Shiloh, Corinth, Arkansas Post, and Vicksburg. He took a column of troops from Fort Smith on Steele's Camden Expedition. He was brevetted major general and mustered out July 19, 1865. He was one of the first senators of Nebraska, governor of Wyoming Territory and governor of Nebraska after the war. Sifakis, *Who Was Who in the Union*, 408.

February 3rd, Wednesday
Had no breakfast except some bean soup. I call that poor fare for a fellow that's on duty every other day. Went to church this evening. Heard a very able discourse.

February 4th, Thursday
Camp full rumors as regards our Regt. leaving Ft. Smith. Nothing definite. Don't know what to do. Nothing to read scarcely.

February 5th, Friday
Moved the camp to north side of Garrison on the river bank. Received a letter from Otis Strong. Oh yes, I had the pleasure of attending an Arkansas dance. A regular HO DOWN. Had a young "lady" to ask me for a "chaw of tobacco".

February 6th, Saturday
On guard at the Garrison on post. No fun guarding Rebel hospital. Went down to town and saw a panorama of the Cutter of the Potomac. Splendid affair indeed.

February 7th, Sunday
Spent the day in camp. Wrote a letter to Otis B. Strong. Weather warm but windy. The steamer LEON arrived tonight from Little Rock loaded with food.[27]

February 8th, Monday
Had battalion drill. The exercises consisted of firing by battalion. This has been a lonesome day.

February 9th, Tuesday
Boat left for below today. One Co. of the 8th Iowa went to Dardanelle, on the boat. Went across the river after flags for our bunks. This has been a

---

[27] Otis B. Strong was the cousin of Henry Strong.

The *Leon* was an eighty-seven-ton stern-wheeler built in 1859 in Brownsville, Pennsylvania. Frederick Way, *Way's Packet Directory, 1848-1994: Passenger Steamboats of the Mississippi River System Since the Advent of Photography in Mid-Continent America* (Athens: Ohio University Press, 1994), 282.

beautiful day. I long to be at home.

February 10th, Wednesday
On guard at the Garrison on Post No. 9, guarding the Battery. Gen. Curtis arrived from Fort Leavenworth this morning. Delivered a speech this evening. All the soldiers and citizens hailed him with joy.[28]

February 11th, Thursday
Grand review of the troops by Gen. Curtis. I was not relieved from duty until three o'clock in the evening. Went fishing this evening. Ha! Fisherman's luck as I usually do. No fish.

February 12th, Friday
Received a letter. On fatigue duty – unloading a train. I am getting tired of staying this out of the way place so long. I'd much rather be moving about. Suppose it is natural for a soldier to be so.

February 13th, Saturday
On guard again at the fort and on camp guard at night. I think this is pretty often for a fellow. Signed the pay rolls today. Will be paid Monday. Rained through the night.

February 14th, Sunday
Company "C" and "G" returned today from Little Rock with a long train of Commissaries. Rained hard nearly all day.

February 15th, Monday
Company paid this morning. Weather warm and pleasant. I did not know what to do so bought a deck of cards. Some of my comrades shook their heads and said a bad idea. But I failed to appreciate the kind advice.

---

[28] Samuel Ryan Curtis was born in New York and raised in Ohio. He graduated from West Point in 1831. He practiced law and became the colonel of the Third Ohio Infantry during the Mexican War. He moved to Iowa where he served three terms in Congress. Curtis was commissioned brigadier general in August of 1861 and commanded the Union Army at Pea Ridge, defeating a larger Confederate force and saving Missouri from the Confederacy. He mustered out April 30, 1866, and died eight months later. Sifakis, *Who Was Who in the Union*, 99.

February 16th, Tuesday
Detailed to go out to a mill seven miles to escort a train after lumber. Loaded and returned before night. Mail failed to arrive last night. Twas robbed near Fayetteville by bushwhackers.

February 17th, Wednesday
Have a big boil on the back of my neck, which interferes with my navigation. Reported on sick list. Guerillas robbed a house on the other side of the river last night.

February 18th, Thursday
Lt. Miserez with twenty five of the Co. started on a foraging trip this morning. Cos. "D" and "F" returned. On sick report. Very cold and dreary. Moved into J. Brown's tent while the boys are gone.[29]

February 19th, Friday
Still on sick report. Am awful lonesome. Cannot run about much. Some very cold weather this week. Mail comes in tonight.

February 20th, Saturday
Nothing unusual today. I am still on sick report. Spent the day in writing. Wrote a letter home.

February 21st, Sunday
Co. "E" started to Fort Gibson this morning to get salt. There are salt works near there. Very pleasant day. Still have a pretty bad sore on my neck.

February 22nd, Monday
Wrote a letter to Libbie and sent by Capt. Bunn as he goes home on furlough. Starts in the morning. Went out to the 2nd Kansas Colored. They drilled for a prize, each company by itself. They are very well drilled. Have been drilling all winter.

February 23rd, Tuesday
I am still under the Dr. charge. Weather very pleasant for this time of the year. Have Battalion drill occasionally.

---

[29]John H. Brown was from Mound City, Kansas, and joined the regiment August 16, 1862. He mustered out June 30, 1865. *Report of the Adjutant General*, 440.

February 24ᵗʰ, Wednesday
Co. "K" returned from foraging trip. Moved camp to out beyond the Catholic Church. Very nice camping place. Sent one dollar to St. Louis for postage stamps, as we can't get them here.

February 25ᵗʰ, Thursday
The General has concluded to fortify Fort Smith. Are going to build a fort near camp. One on the Texas Road and one on the Van Buren. Besides several summits between. Our Regt. at work on the fortifications. Still on sick report.[30]

February 26ᵗʰ, Friday
I am still unfit for duty. The Regt. are put through digging and throwing up (ditches) intrenchment. Wrote a letter to Edward.[31]

February 27ᵗʰ, Saturday
Reported for duty. I was out digging by the Catholic Church. Weather cloudy with appearance of rain. Loaned Eugene Smith three dollars. No news or any excitement. [32]

February 28ᵗʰ, Sunday
On guard today at the Garrison. Rained and sleeted all day. Had a very disagreeable time. Received a letter from Tom Darlow and wrote an answer to send by John Dunbar, who goes home on furlough.

---

[30] By General Curtis' orders, the fortification line eventually extended around the perimeter of the city and included two blockhouses and four firing platforms. Rifle pits or trenches connected the positions, and all timber was cut down on the approaches to town. While the soldiers did most of the work, all able-bodied men and boys were required to labor as well. *The War of the Rebellion: A Compilation of the Official Records of the Union and Confederate Armies*, 4 series, 70 vols. in 128 books and index (Washington: Government Printing Office, 1880-1901), series I, vol. 34, pt. 2, 259 [cited hereafter as *OR*, and unless otherwise indicated, all references are to Series I].

[31] Edward Strong was Henry's brother.

[32] Eugene E. Smith was from Mound City, Kansas, and joined the regiment August 20, 1862. He mustered out, June 30, 1865. *Report of the Adjutant General*, 440.

February 29th, Monday

Mustered for pay today. Ten of the Co. started on foraging trip with Company "A". Regt. are relieved from duty.

March 1st, Tuesday

Weather warm and pleasant. Mail came in today, but no letters for Co. "K". Commenced to board with Peter Eby today. Grub awful scarce.

March 2nd, Wednesday

Nothing of interest in camp today. These are lonesome days for me.

March 3rd, Thursday

On duty today. Working on fortifications. Had much rather do such duty than post duty, as we don't work very hard. Only thirteen dollars per month, and that work or play is sure to come.

March 4th, Friday

Suspended work on the fortifications because rations are so scarce. Reg. Train returned from foraging. The Post Battery moved from the Garrison out to our camp. Suppose Gen. Thayer is working to keep it from Blunt. This is the reason that we were relieved from Post duty, as Gen. Blunt takes part of the Garrison, and he is working hard against Thayer.[33]

March 5th, Saturday

Got a pass and went to town. Mail came last night, but I was so unfortunate as to get nary a letter. Smith's 2nd Kansas Battery moved out by our camp. Several tell of hard feelings between the head officers. Letter advertised for me in the Post Office.[34]

---

[33] Generals Blunt and Thayer were involved in a squabble, which centered on Fort Smith's placement in the Department of Arkansas or the Department of Kansas. Eventually the argument would involve General Grant and President Lincoln. The final solution was that Fort Smith and Indian Territory were assigned to the Department of Arkansas. Thayer remained in Fort Smith. Edwin C. Bearss and Arrell M. Gibson, *Fort Smith: Little Gibraltar on the Arkansas* (Norman: University of Oklahoma Press, 1969) 9-51.

[34] Edward A. Smith was from Fort Scott, Kansas. He was commissioned first lieutenant, Second Kansas Battery, August 25, 1862, and was promoted captain July 4, 1863. He mustered out August 15, 1865. *Report of the Adjutant General*, 628.

March 6th, Sunday

I attended Catholic Church twice today. It is strange what notions different people will get in their heads in regard to religion. Went over to the 2nd Kansas Colored to witness a stylish dress parade. Commissary train arrived from Little Rock.

March 7th, Monday

On fatigue duty. Cleaning off the drill ground. Have to drill from now on. Sgt. Bodel with ten went out ten miles to a mill after meal. Loaned T. Mason two dollars. A boat arrived tonight from Little Rock.[35]

March 8th, Tuesday

Companies "K", "B", and "G" started on a foraging trip. Traveled twelve miles and camped near Vashgrass. Command under Capt. Umbarger, Co. "B" and Co. "K" under Lt. Barrett.[36]

March 9th, Wednesday

Struck the river twenty miles below Fort Smith. Three boats were there unloading Government freight, as the river is so low that they cannot get up to the Fort. Here we turned into the mountains and camped eight miles above Ozark. (Ozark on the north side of the river) and loaded the train and went out one mile from the river and camped for the night. The rest of the teams and command went down the river to hunt a turnip patch. Got lost. Did not find it nor get back to camp until after dark. We killed three big fat hogs. Weaver and I laid out in the brush and watched them all the afternoon. Are going to take them into camp.

---

[35] John Bodel was from Marmaton, Kansas. He joined the regiment September 3, 1862, and was promoted sergeant September 30, 1862. He mustered out June 30, 1865. *Report of the Adjutant General*, 442.

Theophilus Mason was from Mound City, Kansas, and enlisted on August 16, 1862. He was wounded at Jenkins' Ferry April 30, 1864. He mustered out with the regiment June 30, 1865. *Ibid.*, 443.

[36] George W. Umberger was from Clinton, Kansas, and was commissioned second lieutenant of Co. B September 25, 1862. He was promoted captain September 30, 1862. He mustered out with the regiment June 30, 1865. *Ibid.*, 423.

March 11th, Friday
Started on our return to the Fort. Traveled eighteen miles and camped one mile from Charleston. Passed through some very pretty country. Weather very cool, in fact – cold enough for winter.

March 12th, Saturday
Traveled twelve miles and camped on a small creek ten miles from Fort Smith. Passed a train going out with Co. "G" as escort.

March 13th, Sunday
Arrived at camp at noon, unloaded the train. This caused considerable grumbling as tis not customary for the escort to unload. There were five letters for me which I was pleased to receive. Jonathan Broadhead of the company has come down from Leavenworth. Dunbar, Mason and Griffith started home on furlough on the 8th.[37]

March 14th, Monday
Twenty of the Co. started again on a foraging trip. I took a walk today up the Poteau. Was hunting muscle shells. They are in great demand for making rings. Weather rather cool for the sunny South.

March 15th, Tuesday
Received a letter from Libbie. Wrote two. A large Sutler train arrived from Fort Scott. Several acquaintances from Osage are along.

March 16th, Wednesday
Had a drill this morning. Last night was awful cold. Rumor in town that the Rebs are moving up to Waldron. Not credited.

---

[37] Jonathan Broadhead was from Mound City, Kansas, and enlisted August 13, 1862. He was promoted regimental commissary sergeant October 1, 1862. He mustered out with the regiment on June 30, 1865. *Report of the Adjutant General*, 442.

Two Masons were in the Twelfth Kansas: Theophilus Mason (see March 7, 1864 entry) and William E. Mason, who was from Turkey Creek and joined the regiment August 23, 1862. *Ibid.*, 443.

Jesse Griffith was from Turkey Creek, Kansas, and enlisted August 23, 1862. He was discharged with the regiment June 30, 1865. *Ibid.*

March 17th, Thursday

Pleasant day. Nothing of interest in camp. Spent the day in laying around camp as usual.

March 18th, Friday

Some of the Osage boys in camp. Very lonesome day in camp. Have nothing to read.

March 19, Saturday

Co. "K" moved camp to town on Van Buren road beyond the Post Chapel. Our company is to go on post duty again. My postage stamps from St. Louis arrived this morning. Received orders to dispose of all extra baggage and be in readiness to march at short notice. Suppose an expedition is to start South.

March 20th, Sunday

On guard today. Warm and pleasant. Making preparations to start South. Sold my dress coat to Ingram for six dollars. Sent blankets and some other things home by Wilcox, who lives at Mapleton.

March 21, Monday

Relieved from duty by the 1st Arkansas Infantry. Boys returned from foraging. Have orders to be ready to march in the morning. I went out in town this evening to call on a "young Arkansas Lady" as a preliminary to leaving Fort Smith.

March 22, Tuesday

Did not start today as expected. 18th Iowa started out on the Little Rock Road. The 13th Kansas moved up from Van Buren to Garrison the Post while command is gone.

March 23rd, Wednesday

The Co. marched out to the Regt. and got dinner. Then the whole command started out east on the Little Rock road six miles and camped for the night, waiting for the whole outfit to come up. Weather cloudy with appearance of rain. The boys are all in good spirits.

March 24th, Thursday

The Regimental outfit all got up at nine o'clock. Packed up and marched eight miles and camped at one p.m. on lush grass. Commenced to rain just as we got to camp, and rained hard all night. I got pretty wet before we could pitch our tent and get our baggage inside. All are glad to see the rain as the roads today were very dusty and made it very disagreeable marching. "I might with propriety say almost unendurable."

March 25th, Friday
Started at 7 a.m. and marched twelve miles. Camped one mile beyond "Tater Hill" Mound. Rather muddy today, but that is much more preferable than dust. The 2nd Colored came up with us tonight. The rest of the command is ahead.

March 26th, Saturday
Started fifteen minutes before 7 a.m. and marched sixteen miles. Camped at 3 p.m. The train is "stuck in the mud" and did not come up til dark. We will have to march considerably slower in order that the trains and artillery can keep up. Are three miles west of a little town called Booneville. Country is getting to be mountainous. I can't see anything that would entice me to leave a civilized and white man's country to dwell in this wilderness among the rocks and hills where even the sun fails to shine more than eight hours in twenty-four.

March 27th, Sunday
Started at 7 a.m. and marched fifteen miles and camped in the valley of Magazine Mountain. 18th Iowa, 1st Colored, some Cavalry are with us now. Quite an army. The Rebels had better make themselves scarce in these parts. These hills are covered with pine timber. A great many people live among these uninviting hills. I don't admire their taste much. They are mostly women and children. Tis seldom we see an able bodied man in these. Some of them are pleased to see the Feds or appear to be so, and I don't doubt some of their sincerity, while others are afraid of us. Wonder what they think of the darky soldiers. One of the 2nd Kansas Cavalry was straggling behind the command. There was also one Rebel killed today. One of them ran on to our men unawares.[38]

---

[38] Magazine Mountain is the highest point in Arkansas at 2,753 feet above sea level.

March 28th, Monday

All the troops ordered to destroy part of the tents and blankets and clothing. Only one blanket and one extra shirt. The rest all to be burned. Our Co. burned seven tents. It seems a great pity that so much has to be destroyed, but teams cannot haul all. We started with baggage enough to supply three times as many men. It takes some time for a fellow to learn everything. Got ready to start at 1 p.m. and marched only five miles. Did not get to camp either til 7 p.m. Roads are so rough and muddy that the teams can scarcely get along. Stop every five minutes. Came across some honey. We more than went for it.

March 29th, Tuesday

Started at sunrise and marched to Danville. Twelve miles and camped. We passed some very swampy country. Have to make corduroy roads by filling in rails until we make a solid bridge. We make Rebel rails suffer. For several miles there was a ridge on which the road passes. It is only four or five rods wide and a swamp on each side. This natural ridge has the appearance of being thrown up for a road. This is a very cold day for this late –tried to snow a little. We are about seventy five miles from Ft. Smith, and over a hundred to Arkadelphia, where it is the supposition we are going. Our command now consists of eight or nine Regts. And three Batteries, enough we think, for any Rebel command in this part of the country. Are under the command of Gen. Thayer. He appears to be a very fine man. Danville is a small one-horse town on the Petti Jean Creek at the foot of mountains of same name. The town is nearly deserted.

March 30th, Wednesday

Broke camp early this morning and marched to the foot of Petti Jean Mountain and waited for the Regt. in advance to get up the mountain. Had to carry our knapsacks up so to lighten the wagons, that they could be got up. Twas 1 p.m. before we reached the top. The men had to assist in getting artillery up the hill. The mountains are covered with pine forests. Passing over the mountain (tis not as hard work getting down as getting up). We came into Fourche LaFave Valley. It is several miles in width, covered with large pine trees, the largest I ever saw. Quite late when we got to camp, which is on a small creek. Are very tired tonight. Distance twelve miles. Very windy day.

March 31st, Thursday

Started early this morning and crossed the Fourche LaFave River. Most of the command waded. I was fortunate enough to get a chance to ride, which I readily accepted. Water was four feet deep. Then crossed the Fourche Mountains. Tis eight miles over them. Had to carry blankets to the top four miles. I thought it a hard way of serving my country. Higher up in the air than I ever was before. Marched off the mountain and camped in a valley. Got twelve miles. Am tired nearly to death. Report in camp that Price has retreated to Shreveport.

April 1st, Friday
Marched down Fourche LaFave Valley. Crossed several streams. Our Regt. in the rear of whole command. The roads are so swampy that we did not get but eight miles. The train in advance got stuck in the mud at dark, two miles from camping place. So we got supper then started on and dragged along till midnight. Had to carry torches to light up the way so as to keep the road not so dark. At midnight lay down to get a little rest –one mile and a half from the main command. I was on guard last night and today. The boys had to carry knapsacks today for the first time. A good many burned them before they would carry them. Six months ago we would not believe that we would be obliged to carry on our backs all our baggage or leave it behind. Many a soldier burned his extra clothes. Are in Perry County.

April 2nd, Saturday
Started at daylight and marched up to the command and got breakfast. After breakfast followed a valley up to the top of this mountain; crossed and followed down another valley. Crossed some pretty mountain streams. Distance today –twenty miles. Got to camp before sundown. Are in Saline Co. but there are but few families living in this part of the country and all Rebels.

April 3rd, Sunday
Marched twelve miles and camped with in six miles of Hot Springs. I carried my knapsack for the first time today. I was tempted to burn it, but find it is the easiest way of carrying my blanket. Am nearly tired out. Capt. Benter of Co. "C" and Act. Adj. Gen. (acting adjutant general) of our Brigade was found dead this morning between our Regt. and Brigade Hdqtrs. He was shot about 9 p.m. last night while going from Regt. to headquarters. Supposed to have been done by bushwhackers as a charge of buckshot entered his body. One Rebel was killed last night and one today by the scouts. Capt. Benter's body was carried along and buried tonight with military honors. Are

getting across the mountains and roads are much better.[39]

April 4th, Monday

Camp roused at three this morning. Started at daylight and marched twenty-five miles all day long. The boys are pretty tired. Passed through Hot Springs. Tis quite a curiosity. The Springs there are so hot that I could not hold my hand in the water. In times of peace, it was quite a noted place. There are a number of bathing houses there for the sick. The town is between two hills, just wide enough for one street, and houses on both sides. Near here are some noted sulphur springs.

April 5th, Tuesday

Marched twenty miles and camped for the night on a large plantation. Are fifteen miles from Arkadelphia. Passed through Rockport. It has been a pretty town. Is on the Washita River, and is the County Seat of Hot Springs County. Had to wade the Washita River. Tis a pretty large stream, very clear water comes from the mountains that we have crossed. Gen. Steel's command from Little Rock has preceded us one week. He has ten or fifteen thousand men. Have got off the mountains and are in a Rebel country. Mostly pine flats. Some very swampy roads. Our provisions have failed and we have to subsist off the country. Details sent out each day to gather up provisions.

April 6th, Wednesday

Marched fifteen miles and at dark in an old field. Our Regt. in a large peach orchard. Rained a little this evening. Crossed Caddo Creek. Had to wade it, as usual. Grub played out. All we have is what we can gather up in the country. Took the Washington road going direct south. Passed four miles west of Arkadelphia. The 6th Kans. Cal. passed through that place and had a skirmish with a part of Shelby's command this morning. Mules are giving out every day. They were in poor condition when we left Ft. Smith. As soon as one tires out, it is turned out to shift for itself. The country is more thickly settled than any we have passed through heretofore. We are getting into the cotton country. Passed one plantation where there was a million dollars worth of cotton packed up. Some of the boys wanted to fire it, but the General would not permit it.

---

[39]Nick L. Benter was from Osage, Kansas, and was commissioned captain of Co. C September 26, 1862. He was killed April 2, 1864, near Hot Springs, Arkansas. *Report of the Adjutant General*, 425.

April 7th, Thursday

Marched fifteen miles today going toward Washington. Passed through the little one horse town of Spooneville, close where Steel had a fight. His command is one day's march ahead of us. Passed where the Rebs attacked Gen. Steel's forces, Marmaduke and Hindman in front and Shelby in the rear. The command was eight miles long and they thought they could destroy part of the train but failed. I can't learn the number killed. No one seems to know. Passed two houses where Federal and Rebel wounded were both in the same house. The women through the country attend on them. They are well cared for. I should hate to be left in this country behind our command. This has been a very warm day. Commences to rain just as we got to camp. Had to burn all the tents this morning as the mules are tiring out fast. So we have no shelter from the rain.[40]

April 8th, Friday

Rained hard all last night. Missed our tents very much. Blankets got wet and

---

[40] Frederick Steele was a native of New York and graduated from West Point. He was brevetted twice during the Mexican War. He led troops at Wilson's Creek, Vicksburg, Helena, Arkansas Post, and Little Rock. He was promoted major general of volunteers and led a campaign from Arkansas to the Red River in April of 1864. Steele was mustered out on January 1, 1867. He died the following year. Sifakis, *Who Was Who in the Union*, 388.

John S. Marmaduke was from Missouri and graduated from West Point in 1857. He became a colonel in the Missouri State Guard at the beginning of the war. He resigned in 1861 to accept a commission in the Confederate Army. He rose to the rank of major general and killed fellow Confederate General Lucius Walker in a duel in Little Rock in 1863. Marmaduke distinguished himself as a cavalry officer in Arkansas and Missouri. He was captured near Mine Creek in Kansas during Price's Raid in November 1864 and remained a prisoner until the end of the war. He was the last Confederate to be promoted major general and was elected governor of Missouri in 1884. He died in 1887. Shea, *War in the West*, 86.

Thomas C. Hindman was a lawyer from Mississippi and served in the state legislature. He moved to Helena, Arkansas, in 1856 and was elected to the U.S. House of Representatives. He organized the Second Arkansas Infantry in 1861, serving as colonel. He was promoted brigadier general and eventually major general. He led troops at Shiloh, Prairie Grove, and the Atlanta Campaign. He moved to Mexico after the war but came back to Arkansas in 1867. He was an outspoken critic of Reconstruction and was murdered by unknown gunmen in 1868. *Ibid.*, 71.

we have to carry them. Are pretty heavy loads. Started at ten a.m. Marched ten miles. Are nearly up with Steele. Pickets are together tonight. See plenty signs of fighting. Limbs cut off the trees. Cannon balls strewed along the road. It was very slow getting the artillery along today as the country is getting to be quite swampy. Timber mostly pine. Some Osage Orange timber growing natural.

April 9th, Saturday

Left camp at one p.m. and marched to Steele's camp. Seven miles. Crossed the Little Missouri River on a pontoon bridge. Quite a curiosity to one who had never saw such a thing. Swamps on both sides of the river. Had to make corduroy bridges by hauling rails and filling in before we could cross. Steele's command has fighting every day. Had a hard fight when crossing the river. Would not have effected a crossing had he not used strategy by sending his forces up and down the river for several miles so they could not tell where he was laying the pontoon until it was down, and part of the troops across. Then came some hard fighting. The Rebs tried to drive him back, but could not accomplish it. Can see some pretty fresh signs. It makes some of the boys look mild. Gen Steele's command welcomed us with cheers. A general advance is to be made tomorrow. The Rebels are in force on a prairie six miles ahead.

April 10th, Sunday

We did not move camp today. Troops been going to the front all day. Train following the evening. Our division is kept in the rear so as to give us an opportunity to rest, as we have been traveling pretty briskly since leaving Fort Smith. The enemy are only five miles off in force. At five o'clock this evening fighting commenced and was kept up till ten p.m. Very heavy cannonading. Our camp was all excitement, being the nearest we ever was to any engagement. At then this evening the Rebels charged on the 3rd Illinois Battery. An Ohio Regt. was in line there, but the darkness hid them from view, as the Rebels came in range they poured in volley and volley of musketry with great execution, which compelled the Rebels to retire, which ended the fighting for today. I am on camp guard. The chain guard raised an alarm and the whole Division was out in line muster. The country is very level, timbered with pine principally. The roads are very difficult to pass considerable of the way owing to artillery and many trains.

April 11ᵗʰ, Monday
Trains commenced to move up early this morning. Our Regt. in the rear of the whole command. Left camp at noon and moved up to where the trains are corralled four miles on the edge of Prairie DeAnne. Skirmishing and cannonading kept up all day. Only one man killed and one wounded on our side. The Regt. falling back toward Washington, which is twenty miles southwest of us. The Rebs have destroyed all the forage so that we cannot get anything to feed the teams. Rained very hard this evening. We have to "lay on arms" tonight.

April 12ᵗʰ, Tuesday
The Rebels retreated last night, not to be seen this morning. Are evidently getting afraid of us. Command started for Camden at noon today, which is about thirty-five miles distant. Are only seventeen miles from Red River. Crossed Prairie DeAnn six miles and camped on Cyprus Creek. This is the first prairie we have seen since leaving Ft. Smith. Citizens here tell us the Rebel force we have been fighting numbers ten or fifteen thousand. Are in Hempstead County.

April 13, Wednesday
The Command started early this morning. General Thayer's Division left in the rear. Had just eaten dinner and getting ready to start. The Rebels attacked us. They drove in the picket and were in camp before we were aware of their approach. We got into line in a hurry and drove them back three miles. We were in line until dark. Got a good long look at them and heard cannon balls whistling over our heads. Our Regt. did not get in range of the Rebel musketry. Was the hardest kind of artillery firing for a little while. At dark we started up to overtake the command which is eight miles ahead. We were up all night and raining all the time, which made the roads worse and worse. Wagons and artillery got mired in Cypress Swamp, so that by daylight we had got only three miles, wet tired, sleepy and hungry. This swamp is the one that the Rebels expected to find us in when they attacked us, which would have given them the advantage, but they were too fast. We lost several in the fight. Rebel losses were greater according to their own reports.

April 14ᵗʰ, Thursday
Were on the road until 9 p.m. trying to catch up with Steele's rear. Had to pile in logs and rails clear across the Cypress Swamp before trains and artillery could be got over. Managed to get six miles through the day. Country either

swamps or pine flats, and there's not much difference in them in this wet weather. We see no more clear, pretty streams, all sluggish streams, fit only for alligators to live in. Hard tack getting mighty scarce. Dire allowances every day. No chance to make up for deficiency by foraging from the Rebels, as the troops ahead take all. The Rebs seem satisfied with the reception we gave them yesterday, as they have not shown themselves since. We burned two bridges after crossing them so they will not find it very easy to follow us.

April 15th, Friday

Crossed a very bad swamp this morning, one mile across. Took til noon to get our train across. We then came to sand hills, which is much better traveling. At dark, got to a stream over which the bridge is destroyed, and had to ford it. Took nearly all night to get train across. Our Regt. got to the crossroads at ten p.m. fifteen miles from command where we camped to await the coming up of train. Gen. Steele had a fight at these crossroads this morning, which resulted in routing the Rebels. Considerable loss on both sides. Distance fifteen miles. Are in Dallas county.

April 16th, Saturday

Marched twelve miles and camped one mile out of Camden. The advance came into town yesterday morning. Brisk firing kept up for several miles along the roads as the marks on the trees give evidence. The Rebs tried to bother as much as possible so as to give them time to move property out of town. Our Cavalry drove them into and right on through town. They went down the river.

April 17th, Sunday

I went into town today to "look around" a little. I was surprised when I saw the fortifications that we got possession of so easily. There are the best kind of forts here on every side of town, and timber all cut down for one mile around to give artillery fair play. Camden is, or was before the war, a very pretty place on the west bank of the Washita River, one hundred and ten miles south of Little Rock, and sixty miles from Pine Bluff. The Cavalry followed a boat down the river and captured it and brought it back. Twas loaded with corn and sugar. Col. Williams and three of the Regt. started on a foraging expedition, two hundred wagons. Pickets have been skirmishing all day.

April 18th, Monday

I am on camp guard today. The remainder of Co. "K" on grand guard. Heard heavy cannonading this morning out on the Washington road, the very one Col. Williams foraging command went out. Later Old Price's whole command attacked the foragers. He had three brigades and plenty of artillery against two pieces of regts. and six pieces of artillery. The Rebels had a trap for them. The train was loaded and returning, had got to within ten miles of town when they came into this ambush. The Rebs closed in on them from three sides. The fight was very severe. Lasted four or five hours. Our troops fired until their ammunition was expended, then clubbed with their guns and went on – as the Rebels had mixed all up with them. After twas useless to fight longer our boys all that could get away, took to the brush and came into camp. Report is that the Rebels killed all the darkies that fell into their hands, wounded, too. Also the officers over the darkies. Our loss is very heavy considering the numbers engaged. Cannot learn anything accurate yet. The property lost is one Section of Rabb's 2nd Indiana Battery and two of the 6th Kansas Howitizers, and a train of two hundred wagons. The Rebs charged on the darkies three times before breaking their lines, and their force was more than five to one.

April 19th, Tuesday

Stragglers are still coming in. A great many of the wounded crawled out in the brush and lay last night, and managed to get to our pickets this morning. The drums were beat all last night to guide those in the woods to camp. The Rebels refuse to let our men go out with flag of truce to bury our dead. Report is that the reason they will not grant it is because their loss is so much greater than ours they do not want to let it be known how many they have killed. It is said to be more than five to one. They killed after our boys surrendered the wounded that had been put in ambulances. If this is true no punishment is too great for them. Col. Williams and most of the officers of his Regt. have come in. Three Regts. sent out to strengthen the pickets.[41]

April 20th, Wednesday

Train arrived from Pine Bluffs today, and we are in need of it, too, as provisions

---

[41] For a complete account of this action, see Edwin C. Bearss, *Steele's Retreat From Camden and the Battle of Jenkins' Ferry* (Little Rock: Arkansas Civil War Centennial Commission, 1967).

were about to give out. The mules have to divide with us. Corn issued to us in the ear. Had to grind it on an old hand mill, but the greatest trouble was – could not get enough corn. Several of the 5th Kansas Cav. are along. One of them (Carbon) called on me today. The Rebs still refuse to let our men go out to the battlefield. Surgeon Lindsey of our Regt. went out with supplies to attend on the wounded. They still continue to come in. If the Rebs won't let us out to the battlefield, wonder if we have not force enough to make them.[42]

April 21, Thursday

Our Regt. ordered out to escort a train after forage. Started at six this morning. Crossed the Washita on a pontoon bridge. Went out about ten miles and loaded the Brigade train with corn and all the grub we could find, and got back just at dark. Got a good deal of meat and some potatoes. Lots of sugar and molasses. The Rebs tried to get their Cavalry between us and town and capture us. They nearly effected it, too, as they were only three miles away when we got back into the road. But we got back all safe. Gen. Steele is going to cut down our transportation Regimental teams. All turned over but four to Regt. Rumor in camp Banks is defeated on Red River. If so, we will not stay in this country long, but the rumor is not credited. Received two letters by the train from Pine Bluff.[43]

April 22nd, Friday

A detail sent out to the battlefield today. No particulars. Rained some through

---

[42] Henry Carbon was from Mound City, Kansas, and enlisted in the Fifth Kansas Cavalry March 10, 1862. He was captured at Marks' Mills, Arkansas, April 25, 1864. He returned and was mustered out April 18, 1865. *Report of the Adjutant General*, 149.

Thomas Lindsey was from Garnett, Kansas, and was commissioned assistant surgeon on September 30, 1862. He mustered out June 30, 1865. *Ibid.*, 420.

[43] Nathaniel P. Banks was a politician and served in Congress and as governor of Massachusetts before the war. President Lincoln appointed him major general of volunteers. He was routed by Stonewall Jackson in the Shenandoah Valley and earned the nickname "Commissary Banks" by the Confederates who took advantage of the great quantity of supplies lost by his command. Transferred west, he failed miserably in the Red River Campaign. He mustered out August 24, 1864, and was a congressman, senator and U. S. Marshal until his death in 1890. Fred Harvey Harrington, *Fighting Politician: Major General N.P. Banks* (Philadelphia: University of Pennsylvania Press, 1948).

the day. Some troops started for Pine Bluff tonight. There is an abundance of cotton, sugar and molasses in town. The two latter articles the soldiers helped themselves pretty freely.

April 23rd, Saturday
Went all over town today to the forts and graveyard. Some very fine monuments in it. The Dr. sent in for ambulances to bring in the wounded. The Rebs don't want to be troubled. The enemy attempted to destroy a bridge over a stream south of town but failed. Just at sundown received orders to move into town by the forts. Did not get all things moved until midnight, I heard.

April 24th, Sunday
Moved again today only a short distance. Am on camp guard. Last night the boys on picket could hear the Rebel pickets. They had artillery on picket. Could hear them felling timber all night.

April 25th Monday
Very warm day. I had a chill of the ague and was quite sick all the evening. Our camp is among the fallen timber. The Regt. busy all removing burning brush. Our Pickets were done in today. Report in camp that Gen. Salomon's Brigade that started to Pine Bluff with the train is captured at Marks Mill on the Saline River. The enemy are watching us very close, evidently trying to cut off supplies and trying to starve us out. It won't take long to do that judging from what we get now, unless supplies come.

April 26th, Tuesday
Rumor that the whole Southern Confederacy are coming here to whip us out. And I guess it is correct (though doubt the whipping part), as we are to leave here tonight. Started at dark and crossed the Washita on the pontoon bridge. Was on the road all night. Did not get out but four miles daylight. Are going toward Pine Bluff. Before starting burned everything we could not carry in knapsacks. Have to carry all grub we will get until we get to where supplies are. Have five hard tack to the man, also a little bacon and coffee. It's pretty hard for me as I am quite unwell.

April 27th, Wednesday
Kept on until three this afternoon and camped. Are about twenty miles from Camden. This has been a very warm day. A good many of the boys are pretty well worn out with the day's march, no sleep last night and have to

carry all we have. I came to the conclusion that one blanket and an extra shirt was load enough for me so burned the rest. Fifteen miles since daylight.

April 28th, Thursday

Marched sixteen miles and camped at Princeton, a small Arkansas town. Country passed through today is very level and sandy. Thinly settled until close to Princeton. A great many of the boys sick and hardly able to walk. Have to throw away their guns and blankets. I can hardly manage to keep up. Was unwell before leaving Camden. The Rebel Cavalry are following us. Rear guard has been skirmishing all day with them. The train going to Pine Bluff was all captured. Three Regts., one Battery and two or three hundred wagons.

April 29th, Friday

Started at day light this morning and marched eighteen miles and came to the Saline River. Got there at one p.m. Commenced raining then and rained all the afternoon steady. The pontoon was laid and train commenced to cross. By this time the river bottom was a perfect swamp. The road was filled up with teams stalled so that they made slow work crossing the river. The Rebels brought up some artillery and tried to shell the train as it came down in the river bottom, but they did no damage. Had nothing for supper but coffee and bacon tonight. Night was so dark that could not get any more teams across before morning.

April 30th, Saturday

Rained almost all night. Lay on a log to keep out of the water. I am on guard. But did not put out any post. The Regt. marched a half a mile to the rear and laid in a field. Came back where the guard were at daylight and made some coffee for breakfast. About daylight a large force of Rebles that had come up during the night—Kirby Smith, Price and several other generals marched down into the bottom and attacked our forces. Our Regt. was soon ordered to take position on the extreme left. Col. Hayes was shot through the leg at first volley from the Rebels before he had got the Regt. in position. The fight continued til one p.m. Very severe. R. B. Burly was killed. Lt. Miserez and Barrett both wounded in the shoulder, slightly. A. Ball, T. Beltes, A. H. Hooker, T. Mason, J. Weir also wounded. Col. Adams commanding our (2nd) Brigade wounded in arm. Col. Hayes leg was broke, bone shattered badly just above the knee. Had his leg amputated this evening. I was not in line with Regt. as the guard was left behind. Had to carry up ammunition to the line of battle as the teams could not get around in the bottoms. Water was from two to ten inches deep over the battlefield. Rained all the morning. At one p.m. the Rebs drew off, and our forces crossed the river quickly and the pontoon was destroyed. The wagons that were stalled in the mud were cut down and left. Those with the severest wounds left on the other side of the river in charge of Surgeon Stuckslager and fell into the Rebels' hands. We marched up four miles from battlefield and camped for the night. The 2nd Kansas Colored captured a Battery of four guns. They were the only cannon on the field, too. They fired only four or five shots before twas taken from them. The loss in our Regt. killed wounded and missing is seventy eight.[44]

---

[44] Edmund Kirby Smith graduated from West Point in 1845. He lived in Virginia and Florida. He was brevetted captain during the Mexican War and served as an instructor at West Point. He served early in the war under Joe Johnston and was promoted lieutenant colonel and then brigadier general. He was wounded at the first Battle of Manassas. He was promoted to major general and served in Kentucky. He was given command of the Trans-Mississippi Department in 1862. He turned back the Red River campaign of 1864 and finally surrendered his command May 26, 1865. He held various civilian positions with colleges after the war and died March 28, 1893, the last of the surviving full generals of the Confederacy. Sifakis, *Who Was Who in the Confederacy*, 261.

Rufus B. Burley joined the regiment August 26, 1862. He was killed in action at Jenkins' Ferry, Arkansas, April 30, 1864. *Report of the Adjutant General*, 442.

Arthur J. Ball joined the regiment August 13, 1862. He was discharged for disability December 26, 1864, as a result of wounds received at Jenkins' Ferry, Arkansas. *Ibid.*

Thomas Beltes was from Mound City, Kansas, and enlisted September 8, 1862. He mustered out May 26, 1865. *Ibid.*

Alfred H. Hooker was from Marmaton, Kansas, and joined the regiment August 21, 1862. He was wounded at Jenkins' Ferry, Arkansas, April 30, 1864. He mustered out June 30, 1865. *Ibid.*, 443.

Jasper N. Weir was from Wyandotte, Kansas, and joined the regiment May 15, 1863. He mustered out June 30, 1865. *Ibid.*, 444.

Cyrus R. Stuckslager was from Pennsylvania and was commissioned regimental surgeon September 30, 1862. He was captured April 30, 1864, at Jenkins' Ferry, Arkansas, and exchanged June 28, 1864. He mustered out with the regiment June 30, 1865. *Ibid.*, 420.

May 1st, Sunday

All the wounded that were able were sent to Pine Bluff under flag of truce. The command started for Little Rock. Very bad traveling, as there has been so much rain. Marched fifteen miles and stopped at eleven in the night to get a little rest. All we had to eat today is a little wheat, which some of the boys found, and but little of that. All are pretty near tired out. I am sick. Can hardly get along. Every man had to carry from sixty to one hundred rounds. The ammunition train was burned this morning.

May 2nd, Monday

Marched twenty five miles. Did not stop til midnight last night. Consequently got but little sleep as we started early this morning. Are only eleven miles from Little Rock. Had no bread now for three days and tis hard marching. Is enough to kill a fellow. If we had to go five miles farther should staid behind as I was completely tired out. Are getting into a hilly country. Not so difficult marching.

May 3rd, Tuesday

Had some hardtack for breakfast this morning that was sent out from Little Rock. Started early this morning and got to Little Rock at noon. We camped a mile out from town. Was awful well pleased to get to a place where we can get a day or two rest. Went into town in the evening to get something to eat.

Have been starved so long. Little Rock is quite a business place and a pretty town. We hear that from authentic source that Rebel loss at Saline Jenkins Ferry was nine hundred and four (904). Our loss was not quite five hundred (500).[45]

May 4th, Wednesday

Are getting a little rested. I wrote a letter home. Received nine letters on my arrival yesterday. Making up for lost times. Six of us bought a mess outfit and living in a home. Misery is promoted to Capt. as Sears has got to be Major of the 77th U.S. Colored. Barrett is 1st Lt. and Orderly Cook 2nd Lt.

---

[45]For a complete description of this action, see Daniel E. Sutherland, "1864: 'A Strange, Wild Time'" in Mark Christ, ed., *Rugged and Sublime: The Civil War in Arkansas* (Fayetteville: University of Arkansas Press, 1994), 110-123.

Their commissions were received today.[46]

May 5th, Thursday
Went to town, also to General Hospital. Saw A. H. Hooker. He is getting along finely, was shot through the leg.

May 6th, Friday
Staid in camp all day. Wrote two letters. Our Division was ordered to march at six p.m. Marched down through town. Bands playing, colors flying, to the levee. Were sent across the river on steamboats and camped near the depot. Twas near midnight before the whole command got across. Are to go back to Fort Smith.

May 7th, Saturday
Drew rations and got ready to march. Have to carry three days rations in haversacks. Went down to the depot to see the train go out. Several boats at the landing are coming and going all the time. Wrote a letter to Libbie. Started at one p.m. for Fort Smith. Marched out four miles and camped for the night. Country begins to look natural again. See oak timber once more, not all pine and cypress. Passed some earth works that the Rebels had thrown up before Little Rock fell.

May 8th, Sunday
Marched fifteen miles and camped on a small stream near the Arkansas River. Am quite unwell today. Could not keep up with the command. Got into an ambulance towards night and to camp five miles. If it had not been for this, should staid behind, as I could not have walked. All the men that were not able to march before leaving Little Rock were put on a boat and sent up to Fort Smith by water. If I had known I should have been so unwell, I would have went on the boat, but I thought I would be able to march with the command.

May 9th, Monday
Marched eighteen miles and camped on Cadron at the mouth of it on the

---

[46] The Kansas Adjutant General's Report states that these promotions occurred May 20. In addition John J. Sears is listed as major, Third Regiment Missouri Colored Volunteer Infantry. *Report of the Adjutant General*, 442.

Arkansas River. Crossed Cadron on a ferry boat. Stopped at noon and got dinner. Rained all forenoon so that was very muddy.

May 10ᵗʰ, Tuesday

Rained hard all last night. Most of the boys got a good wetting as we have no tents and most of the boys threw away their blankets as they could not carry them. I am no better. Can hardly get along. Kept along the brink of the river. Fifteen miles. Rained so much that it is very bad marching. Got to Lewisburg at noon and camped for the night as to draw rations. This place is a military post. A good many troops stationed here. Our Regt. transferred to 1ˢᵗ Brigade Col. Edwards, Commander.[47]

May 11, Wednesday

Marched eighteen miles. Camped this side of the river. Three boats tied up by camp for the night that are bound for Fort Smith. Gen. Thayer is aboard. Stopped in the middle of the day and got dinner and rested.

May 12ᵗʰ, Thursday

Marched twelve miles and got to opposite Dardenelle at noon and camped. There are troops stationed at Dardenelle. It is half way between Little Rock and Fort Smith. All the command crossed on Steamboats except "K" and "F" Cos. of the 12the Kansas and two Cos. of the 1ˢᵗ Artk Infty., which are to go up on this side of the river with the train.

May 13, Friday

Marched twenty three miles and camped on Piney. Passed through Russellville four miles from Dardenelle and struck out into the hills. Very rough country. Thinly settled. Crossed Illinois Bayou, quite a large stream. Have to wade it, but tis not as cold as streams were when we started out, so don't mind it.

May 14ᵗʰ, Saturday

Started at sunrise and marched twenty miles. Passed through Clarksville. Stopped three miles this side of town and got dinner.

---

[47] John Edwards was colonel of the Eighteenth Iowa Infantry and placed in command of the post of Fort Smith in January of 1864 until it was transferred to General Thayer. He was promoted to brigadier general and commanded the First Brigade, Third Division, Seventh Corps, Army of the Frontier. Carolyn Pollan, "Fort Smith Under Union Rule: September 1, 1863-Fall, 1865," *The Journal* 6 (April 1982): 24-28.

May 15ᵗʰ, Sunday
Marched twenty miles and camped on White Oak, thirty miles from Van Buren. Crossed a number of mountain streams. Mountains in sight all day to the north of us. Left Ozark five miles to the left. We are getting along pretty rapidly. At night I am pretty tired when night comes.

May 16ᵗʰ, Monday
Marched twenty-six miles and camped four miles from Van Buren. Crossed Big and Little Mulberry and Big and Little Frog Bayou.

May 17ᵗʰ, Tuesday
Got to Van Buren at 8 a.m. Took all day to get the train across. Then marched five miles and got to Smith just at dark. Gen. Thayer and command arrived yesterday. Capt. Burns just returned from home. He brought me two letters.

May 18ᵗʰ, Wednesday
Went into camp on the east side of the Catholic Church in an old field. Looked about town a little today. Everything looks quite natural. Found Tom Darlow here working in the Government. Stopped and had a long chat with him concerning old times past. Wrote several letters. Have to make up for lost time, now that I have leisure time.

May 19ᵗʰ, Thursday
They are fortifying the town. All the citizens are out cutting down the timber. Our Regiment dug riflepits in front of our camp. Marmaduke and Shelby have taken Dardenelle. Our troops are to be withdrawn from Clarksville, and the Rebels are getting pretty numerous in these (days) since our Army had retreated back. The report is that they crossed the river and are going north, probably to Missouri.

May 20ᵗʰ, Friday
Went down town. Plenty of rumors in circulation in regard to Rebels coming this way. Are busily engaged in throwing up fortifications.

May 21ˢᵗ, Saturday
I am on Camp guard today. A very heavy detail on fatigue duty from the Regt., digging trenches and felling timber.

May 22, Sunday

I attended Catholic church this morning. Quite a novelty to see them go through their various ceremonies. Wrote a letter then went down town and staid all night with Tom Darlow.

May 23, Monday

Showery. Rumor in camp that Gen. Grant has driven the Rebels inside of their fortifications at Richmond, and captured large numbers of prisoners and artillery and ammunitions of war.

May 24th, Tuesday

Am on fatigue, digging on the rifle pits. Are getting along finely with the work. The report of Col. Cloud ripping out the Rebels down at Sugar Loaf Mountain confirmed. Capt. Gibbons of the Militia killed by bushwhackers at his home, six miles from town.[48]

May 25th, Wednesday

Our Regt. received marching orders. Were after countermanded. Are sent as funeral escort to bury Capt. Gibbons. Two of the Co. started to Fort Gibson on the Sunny South as escort.[49]

May 26th, Thursday

On fatigue duty working on riflepits. Our rations are getting scarce, so we did not do much.

May 27th, Friday

Various reports in camp as to our leaving here. Don't care how soon that happens as we don't get rations enough. Our mess had to buy flour today. Are going to quit doing duty unless we get more rations.

---

[48]William F. Cloud was from Emporia, Kansas, and was commissioned colonel June 20, 1861. He had a reputation as a capable officer and led troops throughout Missouri, Kansas, Arkansas and Indian Territory. Cloud mustered out January 19, 1865, at Fort Leavenworth. *Report of the Adjutant General*, 78.

James Gibbons, captain, Co. B, Arkansas Militia, is buried in the Fort Smith National Cemetery. "Northern Troops in Fort Smith, 1863," *The Journal* 5 (April 1981): 27-33.

[49] The *Sunny South* was a 270-ton side-wheeler built in 1860 in Wheeling, Virginia. Way, *Way's Packet Directory*, 437.

May 28th, Saturday

Spent the rest of this month looking around. Wrote several letters home. 29th, 30th, 31st.

June 1st, Wednesday

Some of the Co. went across the river fishing to a large lake. Had good success. Lots of fish. I am on picket guard. Report that there has been a fight at Pine Bluffs. Not much news. From the 1st to the 15th of the month spent in camp and on duty. Boats coming and going all the time. Are bringing up commissaries pretty.

June 15th, Wednesday

Twenty-five of the Regt., myself included, under command of Lt. Cook started to Fort Gibson on the Steamer J. R. Williams. We got down finely til four p.m. Passed Fort Coffee on a high point on the south side of the river. This is where the Rebel Col. Coffee and his command at the commencement of the war, fortified the bluff. But when the Federals took possession of this country, they left their fortress without waiting to be forced. At four p.m., fifty miles above Fort Smith and near the mouth of the Canadian, a force of Rebels under Cooper, attacked the boat from the south bank of the river with artillery, four pieces. They soon disabled the boat, which the pilot ran to opposite side, or as near as the shallow water would permit. The engineer and fireman were killed at the second or third shot and the boat disabled. The escort got behind the freight and returned the fire to the best advantage we could. When the Rebels opened fire on the boat I was sitting up on the hurricane deck, but I got below as soon as possible and got my gun. As soon as the Lt. saw that it would be folly to stay on the boat longer, as we would all be killed, he ordered us to leave the boat. It was about forty yards from this boat to the water's edge, and three or four hundred across the sandbar to timber, where we would be safe from the Rebel fire. At the command we all jumped overboard, water waist deep and waded ashore, then across the bar to the woods where we all reached. Two of the boys, only, being wounded, not dangerous either. The Rebs kept up a most terrific fire, until we got out of sight, with both artillery and small arms and some of their balls came pretty close to a fellow, so Lt. Cook decided to stay under cover of the woods until night, and then venture back to the boat, and if it could not be got away, to fire it. With our rifles, we could prevent any of them coming over to the boat. But just as the Lt. had decided what course to pursue, the Capt. of the boat and Lt. Huston, who had hid in the hull of the boat when the firing took place, came out from their hiding place and took the boat, and went over to the Rebels. Now they had the means of coming to the boat, and we could not prevent it. So we started for Fort Smith, as we had nothing to eat and no one living between this and the Fort. At five o'clock we started taking a northeast course through the woods and some brooks. At sundown we came onto a large prairie. None of us were ever in this part of the country before. We laid down in the grass to wait until dusk for fear there might be a bank of Rebels on this side of the river, and could see us a long distance. At dusk, we resumed our march, keeping in the same course, intending to strike the Ft. Smith and Gibson road before morning. We came to this road at ten o'clock and followed it towards Smith, using the utmost caution. Not a man spoke above a whisper the whole night. Crossed a number of streams, which were swelled to unusual size owing to the recent rains. When we got fatigued that we could not possibly go any farther, would lie down and rest a few minutes.[50]

June 16th, Thursday
Kept on this morning until 9 a.m. and came to the Govt. outpost nine miles from Smith, when some of the 9th Kansas were there they got us some breakfast, which we done ample justice to, having had nothing since noon the day before and marched during that over forty miles. After resting a while, we started on and got to comp at three p.m., tired, wet and sleepy. Were out in some of the hardest showers there has been this year. Well, it rained enough to raise the Arkansas River ten feet in two days. The boys that were barefoot had been all cut up with gravel and swelled up awfully, big as three or four natural sized feet. A detachment was sent up the river after the Rebels. But there has been so much rain and high water that they cannot effect any gain. Barrels of flour and other articles are floating the river.

---

[50] Douglas H. Cooper was from Mississippi and fought in the Mexican War with his close friend, Jefferson Davis. In 1853 he was appointed as federal agent to the Choctaw Nation. At the beginning of the war, he was commissioned by the Confederacy to cultivate support among the tribes. He became colonel of the First Choctaw and Chickasaw Mounted Rifles and participated at Pea Ridge and later at Honey Springs in Indian Territory. He was promoted brigadier general in 1863 and replaced Samuel Bell Maxey as commander of Indian Territory in February of 1865. He died in the Chickasaw Nation in 1879. John C. Waugh, *Sam Bell Maxey and the Confederate Indians* (Fort Worth, TX: Ryan Place Publishers, 1995).

Stand Watie actually led the attack on the steamboat. *OR*, vol. 34, pt, 1, 1013-1061.

June 17th and 18th, Friday and Saturday

From the boat (JR Williams), several barrels caught by the boys. The river is in splendid condition for boats. Several up from Little Rock. Nothing of importance during the remainder of the month occurred. I was not able for duty for a week or ten days after my boat excursion.

July 1st, Friday

Nothing worthy of note, but are taking advantage of the high water and bringing up a big supply of commissaries. This month passed quietly with the usual routine of duty. Have a great deal of duty to do working on fortification. Was paid off on the 23rd of July, but six months' pay. Sixteen dollars per month since the 1st of May.

July 27th, Wednesday

The 6th Kansas attacked by two thousand Rebels this morning about sunrise. The 6th were camped on Massard Prairie sight from town. Eleven were killed; sixteen wounded and over one hundred taken prisoners. Ten of the

---

Fort Coffee was located six miles north of Spiro, Oklahoma, in LeFlore County. The fort was established in 1834 to halt the liquor trade in Indian Territory. The fort was named for a former paymaster of the Army and abandoned in 1838. Odie B. Franks, Kenny Arthur Franks, and Paul L. Lambert, *Early Military Forts and Posts in Oklahoma* (Oklahoma City: Oklahoma Historical Society, 1978).

John T. Coffee was from Missouri and became a colonel in the Confederate Army. He commanded a cavalry regiment. *OR*, vol. 22, pt. 1, 903-932.

The *J. R. Williams* was loaded with 16,000 pounds of bacon, 150 barrels of flour and a quantity of tinware. On the return trip, the boat was scheduled to bring salt and lime back to Fort Smith. For a complete account of this action, see David Stephen Heidler, Jeanne T. Heidler, and David J. Coles, *Encyclopedia of the American Civil War: A Political, Social, and Military History* (Santa Barbara, CA: ABC-CLIO, 2000), 1096-1097 and *Sam Bell Maxey and the Confederate Indians*, 67-70.

George W. Huston was from Leavenworth, Kansas, and was commissioned lieutenant, regimental quartermaster for the Fourteenth Kansas Cavalry, October 17, 1863. He was a prisoner of war until May 27, 1865. He was mustered out with the regiment June 25, 1865. *Report of the Adjutant General*, 471.

General Thayer described the conduct of Second Lieutenant Cook as unjustifiable and a criminal abandonment of duty. He recommended that Cook be dismissed from service. *OR*, vol. 34, pt. 4, 504-564.

Rebels killed, four wounded and brought into the hospital. Several taken prisoners. The 6th Kansas fought them until overpowered, refusing to surrender until all surrounded.[51]

July 29th, Friday

Four bushwhackers shot today who were captured near Fayetteville. Our Regt. and the colored Regt. out under arms.[52]

July 31st, Sunday

This afternoon the enemy drove in the pickets on the Texas Road and commenced shelling Post No. 2. The 2nd Kansas Battery were soon playing on them pretty lively and forced them to fall back. Considerable firing with artillery. The Rebs came down between Poteau and the Arkansas River and shelled the garrison, but did no damage. Our batteries played on them so lively that they had to retreat back out of range.[53]

---

[51] For a complete account of Massard Prairie, see Steve Cox, "*The Action on Massard Prairie*," *The Journal* 4 (April 1980): 11-13.

[52] A.J. Copeland, James H. Rowton, John Norwood, and William Carey were executed by a detail of the Thirteenth Kansas Infantry. They had been convicted in the murder of John Brown, a citizen of Fayetteville, Arkansas, and eight soldiers of the First Arkansas Cavalry (Union). The four men, with accomplices, had disguised themselves as Federal soldiers and committed the murders. A military commission was convened in Fayetteville April 14, 1864, to rule on the case. William Furry, ed., *The Preacher's Tale: The Civil War Journal of Rev. Francis Springer, Chaplain, U.S. Army of the Frontier* (Fayetteville: University of Arkansas Press, 2001), 109-126.

[53] The attack on Fort Smith was a continuation of the action started on July 27, 1864, at Massard Prairie. The combined command of Watie and Gano probed the garrison of Fort Smith for six days. While the Rebels were not successful in retaking the post, they forced thousands of refugees into the city, further straining the already taxed Federal supply line. *OR*, vol. 41, pt. 1, 25-83.

Richard M. Gano was from Kentucky. He was a physician and before the war moved to Texas. At the beginning of the war, he served with John Hunt Morgan as colonel of the Seventh Kentucky Cavalry. He was assigned to the Trans-Mississippi and promoted brigadier general by General Edmund Kirby Smith. He returned to Texas after the war where he became a minister in the Christian Church. He died in Dallas March 27, 1913. Waugh, *Sam Bell Maxey and the Confederate Indians*, 72.

August 1ˢᵗ, Monday

Had quite an exciting time on picket last night. Could hear the Rebels moving round to the southeast side of town in the night. We expected them in on us at daylight, but they failed to come. At daylight firing commenced over cross Poteau and was continuous at intervals through the day. At night the Rebs disappeared and was seen no more. The next day, our company sent over Poteau to cut down the timber so as artillery could have fair play. All the refugees are moving over nite from town. One of Co. "B" shot himself and one other accidentally. One of them died. None of the boys are allowed to leave the Regt.[54]

August 10ᵗʰ, Wednesday

One of Co. "B", 12 Kansas, who was taken prisoner at Jenkins' Ferry last April escaped from the Rebels four miles from Tyler. He came into town today, played off "Butternut" on all the rebel forces he came across and got through safe. The 18ᵗʰ Iowa came up today from below. Considerable rain nowadays. The mail coming from Fayetteville was captured by Rebels and Harrison Stevens of the 6ᵗʰ Kansas, one of the escort, killed. Also several others. There are a great many rumors afloat in regard to the Regt. going to Fort Scott. Nothing of importance until August 24ᵗʰ.[55]

August 24ᵗʰ, Wednesday

The Rebels under Gano attacked the 11ᵗʰ Colored this morning at daybreak, which is stationed out on the Gibson Road twelve miles from here. There were five hundred Rebels and only two hundred of the darkies. The Rebels charged into camp just at daylight, driving in the pickets, and were in camp before the darkies were aware of their approach. The darkies soon drove them out of camp. The Rebs formed again and tried to charge the camp

---

[54] Jesse Hale was from Lawrence, Kansas, and enlisted August 15, 1862. He was killed by accidental discharge August 1, 1864. *Report of the Adjutant General*, 424.

[55] Thomas Pugh was from Willow Springs, Kansas, and enlisted May 20, 1862. He was promoted to corporal October 1, 1862. He was captured at Jenkins' Ferry, Arkansas, April 30, 1864. He is listed as having escaped from Camp Ford in Texas by researcher Vicki Betts from the University of Texas at Tyler. *Ibid.*, 430.

William H. Stevens was from Twain Springs, Kansas, and enlisted September 2, 1862, in Co. E, Sixth Kansas Cavalry. He was killed in action August 12, 1864, near Van Buren, Arkansas. *Ibid.*, 181.

again, but backed as the darkies were ready for them. The 11th were out there guarding haymakers. The Rebs fired all the hay that was put up, but did not damage much as twas most all hauled in to the Fort. As soon as it was learned that the Rebs were on the prairie, our Regt. was ordered out to the scene of action. Arrived at three p.m. but the enemy had crossed the Arkansas River and off. Surgeon Gen. was killed and four colored soldiers. John Parks of our Co. captured –was teamster. One of the Rebels was killed in camp, a Choctaw Indian.[56]

August 25th, Thursday

This morning our Regt. was ordered on toward Fort Gibson to meet the train. Was expected in and strengthened the escort. Had no blankets as we did not expect to go out farther than the 11th Camp when we left town. Marched fifteen miles and camped on Salisaw and got supper. Started at dark and marched four miles further and camped on the prairie. Rather cold lying out in the night dew with no blankets. Rebs got the worst of the fight yesterday.

August 26th, Friday

Started at daylight and marched two miles to Little Bayou, and got breakfast. Then marched nine miles farther to Big Bayou, and camped for the night. Crossed a big mountain. Very hot day. One of Co. "E" sunstruck while on the mountain. Crossed a very large prairie today. Sent a dispatch to Gibson to send us rations. Are about thirty-five miles from that place.

August 27th, Saturday

Rained last night. Laid on the "dry side" of a rail. All got a good wetting. Started at 4 p.m. and marched eight miles to the Salt Works on the Illinois River, in among the hills, hardest kind of a looking place. All the salt used by the Army in this part of the country is made here. Capt. Bruce with a detachment of Indians are stationed here and making salt. The Salt Spring is in the middle of Illinois River. Can tell the saltwater from the fresh by the color of it.[57]

---

[56] John H. Parks was from Mound City, Kansas, and enlisted September 5, 1862. He was captured in the Cherokee Nation August 25, 1864. He mustered out July 15, 1865. *Report of the Adjutant General*, 443.

[57] James H. Bruce was commissioned captain May 27, 1863, in the Second Regiment Indian Home Guard. Previously he had been first lieutenant in the Fourth Kansas Infantry. *Ibid.*, 9.

August 28ᵗʰ, Sunday
Rained hard this morning. Train came in from Gibson. Went up on the mountain and camped. Four miles from Salt Works on our return.

August 29ᵗʰ, Monday
Marched fifteen miles and camped on Little Bayou. Very difficult getting over the rough hilly country.

August 30ᵗʰ, Tuesday
Marched twenty miles and camped one mile beyond the 11ᵗʰ U.S. Colored's camp. Boys sent our rations to us from the Fort. Morgan came down from Fort Scott with the train. He has not been with the Company since we were at Fort Leavenworth.[58]

August 31ˢᵗ, Wednesday
Got to camp before night. Four companies are to stay on the Sallisaw to guard the haymakers. Tis thirty miles from Fort Smith. Quite a long distance to haul hay I think. Josiah Rhoton died while we were gone. I sent to New York City for some books.[59]

September 1ˢᵗ, Thursday
Companies "B" and "K" ordered back across the river last night to guard the train until it is crossed over. Stayed here all day. Received a letter from Libbie. Very warm weather. Have great times in the river bathing.

September 2ⁿᵈ, Friday
Came across to the camp this afternoon. Two of the 1ˢᵗ Arkansas killed by bushwhackers.

---

[58] Dozier T. Morgan was from Mound City, Kansas, and enlisted August 16, 1862. He was promoted corporal September 30, 1862. He mustered out with the regiment on June 30, 1865. *Ibid.*, 442.

[59] Josiah Rhoton was from Marmaton, Kansas, and enlisted August 16, 1862. He died of chronic diarrhea in Fort Smith, Arkansas, August 27, 1864. He is buried in the National Cemetery in Fort Smith. *Ibid.*, 443.

September 5th, Monday

Our Co. sent down the river ten miles to escort a train after corn. Went into the field and gathered it and got back before night. Nothing unusual occurred for several days. A great many rumors current in regard to Rebels crossing the river and going north, crossing at Ozark and below.

September 11th, Sunday

Our Regt. ordered across the river or all that are able to march. Crossed over this evening and camped near the river bank.

September 12th, Monday

Left camp this morning and marched out to the 11th U.S. colored camp twelve miles and camped for the night. Had battalion drill. The boys all grumbled a great deal. The Col. told them to dry it up, threatening pretty hard if they did not. Some scout came dashing into camp at John Gilpin speed, raising quite an alarm. Regt. got into him.[60]

September 13th, Tuesday

Marched fifteen miles and camped on the prairie near Sallisaw. Met a sutler train going to Fort Smith. Report that there are three hundred rebels near the 11th's old camp.

September 14th Wednesday

Started at light and marched to Sallisaw and got breakfast. Then to where the haymakers are camped three miles farther. Some one (supposed to be Rebels) broke all the mowing machines last night. So work will be suspended or until they can be replaced. This Battalion that arrived today relieved the 11th Colored and they are going to Gibson. Thirty of our Regt. are detailed to go along to bring rations back. Myself included. Lt. McArthur in command. Marched eleven miles and camped four miles from Salt Works.[61]

---

[60] The phrase "John Gilpin Speed" comes from a poem written in 1782 by British poet William Cowper entitled *The Diverting History of John Gilpin*. The poem is an epic comedy, which centers on the traveling misfortunes of John Gilpin. Gilpin rides his horse recklessly because he is late for an appointment. The phrase came to mean someone riding or moving recklessly. William Cowper, *The Diverting History of John Gilpin* (New York: E.P. Dutton, 1899).

[61] Alexander McAuthor was from Hyatt, Kansas, and was commissioned first lieutenant

September 15ᵗʰ Thursday
Marched fifteen miles and camped on Greenleaf Prairie. Nine miles from Gibson Road. Not so hilly this side of Ill. River.

September 16ᵗʰ, Friday
Marched nine miles and got to Fort Gibson at ten o'clock. Some four hours before the 11ᵗʰ did. Made preparations to start back early in the morning. Were ordered not to go tomorrow as the Rebels attacked a hay party out on Flat Rock today. Killed a good many and burnt the hay. Did not learn the particulars tonight.

September 17ᵗʰ, Saturday
Our little detachment moved into the Fort last night. One Co. of 2ⁿᵈ Kansas Cavalry and one of 1ˢᵗ Kansas colored were camped out there guarding the haymakers. The report today is that they are nearly all killed and taken prisoners. Last night was one of intense excitement. All the Indians were turned out and armed and preparations made to repel an attack. Sent to Smith for reinforcements, also, down on the prairie where our Regt. is.

September 18, Sunday
Troops sent out all last night to pursue the Rebels who are estimated at five thousand under Gano. They are going north toward Cabin Creek. Fears are entertained about the Govt. train coming from Fort Scott, which is supposed to be near Cabin Creek. Our detachment of thirty is all that are in the Fort. Col. Williams and 1ˢᵗ and 54ᵗʰ Colored came in today. Were put in wagons and started out after the Rebels, who are reported to be out about thirty miles. All the refugee Indians here have been armed to help defend the Post in a case of emergency. Spent the day with John Wheaten, who is here. Our boys went out to Flat Rock to bury the dead. Found twenty-one dead darkies belonging to the 1ˢᵗ Kansas Colored. The Rebels slaughtered all they could catch. Several of the 2ⁿᵈ Kansas Cavalry were killed, but they had a better chance to get away, being Cavalry.

September 19ᵗʰ, Monday
The Rebels attacked the train on Cabin Creek at one o'clock this morning, before any of the reinforcements sent out could (did) get there to render any

in Co. G, Twelfth Kansas Infantry September 30, 1862. He was promoted to captain March 22, 1865, and mustered out June 30, 1865. *Report of the Adjutant General*, 434.

assistance. After fighting, several of our forces were obliged to give it up, as the Rebs had artillery and used it with telling effect on the escort. They left the train some going direct for Fort Scott and footmen taking out into the hills intending to reach this place. There seems to be some mismanagement on the part of the Commanding Officer, as he was aware of the train being on the way, and with small escort. He had time to send reinforcement to the train before the Rebels could get there, if he had started them as soon as Gano crossed the Arkansas River. This will be a severe loss as rations are very low here and Fort Smith also. This place depends entirely on Ft. Scott for supplies.[62]

September 20th, Tuesday
Our Regt. came in this morning having marched all last night. Are pretty well tired out from appearance, I should judge. Col. Adams assumed command of the post as soon as he arrived.

September 21st, Wednesday
Col. Williams and command returned from the chase today. He came up with Gano's rear and shelled them awhile, but they were Cavalry and could soon get out of his way. The loss was very heavy – about two hundred and fifty Government wagons loaded with clothing and commissaries, also one hundred or more private teams loaded with sutler goods.

September 22nd, Thursday
Major Kennedy with the boys that were left at Fort Smith came in today. Brought the mail. I received a letter from Cousin Otis. Wind blew awful hard today. Our Regt. is all together once more.[63]

September 23rd, Friday
Williamson of our Co. started home this morning. I sent seventy-two dollars by him and some letters. Our Regt. ordered back to Fort Smith. Started and

---

[62] The raid at Cabin Creek by Confederate forces under Watie and Gano netted an estimated one and a half million dollars worth of supplies. The loss was greatly felt over the coming winter at Fort Gibson and Fort Smith. Waugh, *Sam Bell Maxey and the Confederate Indians*, 71-80.

[63] Thomas H. Kennedy was from Lawrence, Kansas, and was commissioned major September 30, 1862. He mustered out with the regiment June 30, 1865. *Report of the Adjutant General*, 420.

marched out 3 miles and camped for the night.[64]

September 24th, Saturday
Marched eleven miles and camped for the night in an old field among the hills. A large train going from Gibson to Fort Smith are with us.

September 25th, Sunday
I was on picket guard last night. Had a great time of it – the Col. going the grand rounds to see if we know our duty. Started at sunrise and marched fifteen miles. Camped on Big Bayou for the night. A great number of the boys are sick from hard marching, coming to Gibson in such a hurry.

September 26th, Monday
Marched fifteen miles and camped near Little Sallisaw. Just at sundown Col. Adams received a dispatch from Gen. Thayer that there was force on the other side of the river and he feared we would be attacked – to come right on through without delay. So started and marched till two o'clock in the morning. Then stopped to get a little sleep eight miles from Ft. Smith. Had a very hard night's march as twas very dark.

September 27th, Tuesday
Started on after a little rest and got to Ft. Smith at noon and went into camp. Had one of the hardest rains this morning while out on the prairie this morning. One of the hardest rains I have been in since in the service. A forage train captured yesterday, part of the escort killed and wounded.

September 28th, Wednesday
Nothing unusual happened during the remainder of this month.

October 1st,
Nothing of importance happened the fore part of this month. Tom Darlow started home. I sent some letters by him. I was unwell for about three weeks. Quite sick. Staid at Dunbars'. Mrs. Dunbar took care of me while sick. Nixon Blair started home on sick furlough. He died near the Salt Works on the road to Gibson on the 22nd of the month. Some of our boys

---

[64] James Williamson was from Marmaton, Kansas, and joined the regiment August 25, 1862. He was promoted corporal September 30, 1862. He mustered out July 14, 1865. *Ibid.*, 443.

went across Poteau and were attacked by Choctaw Indians (Rebels). One of Co. "A" killed, one of 13th Kansas and two of the 18th Iowa. The killed were scalped. Some of our company ran a very narrow escape. A great many rumors afloat in regard to Rebels going north, probably Missouri. The Regt. is building winter quarters.

Carpenter died on the 25th. Was buried with Masonic and Military honors. We hear that old Price with twenty-five thousand men are at or near Lexington, Missouri, and going toward Kansas.

On the 31st our Regt. crossed the river. Reported that eight hundred Indians crossed Ark. River going north.[65]

November 1st, Tuesday
Marched out from town nine miles but could see no sign of Rebels so returned to town. Rained hard today.

November 4th, Friday
News of a fight in Kansas somewhere in Linn County reached here today. Am very anxious to hear particulars.[66]

November 5th, Saturday
Our Regt. and the 54th U.S. Colored ordered to Van Buren. It is reported that Price's forces are coming this way. They are reported to have been whipped out in Kansas and retreating this way closely persued. News came in tonight that Blunt fought them at Newtonia, Mo.

---

[65] Nixon Blair was from Marmaton, Kansas, and enlisted August 16, 1862. He died of disease in Fort Scott, Kansas, October 10, 1864. *Report of the Adjutant General*, 442.

Chester B. Carpenter was from Mound City, Kansas, and enlisted August 16, 1862. He died of fever in Fort Smith, Arkansas, October 25, 1864. *Ibid.,* 443.

William Whitefeather was from Wyandotte, Kansas, and enlisted in Co. A, Twelfth Kansas Infantry August 22, 1862. He was killed by guerillas near Fort Smith, Arkansas, October 22, 1864. He is buried in the National Cemetery at Fort Smith. *Ibid.,* 422.

[66]The action in Linn County was the end of Price's Raid.

November 6th, Sunday
Staid at Van Buren until sundown, then marched back to Fort Smith. Some of the Colored Regts. went up the river a few miles. Price's forces crossing at Webber's Falls, going south as fast as possible.

November 7th, Monday
Four Regts. of Cavalry came in from Little Rock today with Gen. Herron, who is on an inspection tour. A large train enroute for this place from Little Rock. Col. Edwards of the 1st Iowa promoted to Brig. Gen.

November 8th, Tuesday
Is election day. All the troops permitted to vote. 1st Ark. Infty. marched out last night, and we had to take their place on picket. Very cold day.

November 9th, Wednesday
Gen. Blunt came into town tonight. He persued Price to the Ark River. They crossed at Webber's Falls, forty miles above here and went into Dixie "pell mell". When they crossed the Ark River, they had only two pieces of artillery. All the rest being captured. Also lost a great many prisoners.[67]

November 10th, Thursday
All the Kansas troops marched down into town this evening, and Gen. Blunt made a speech giving an account of Price's raid in Kansas and the fight of Big and Little Blue, Westport, Trading Post, Mine Creek and Newtonia and pursuit to the Ark River. He was followed by several other speakers, and then marched back with cheering and other manifestations of joy. The 11th Kansas Cav. are here. All the other troops turned back to Ft. Scott. If this affair had been managed right, Price could never got back across the Ark River as easily as he did. Gen. Thayer should have sent troops out to the crossing as soon as he learned where Price would cross, and prevented it, which could have been done. Is the general opinion.

November 12th, Saturday
Gen. Herron reviewed the troops today. One of the 11th Kansas over in camp. He is acquainted with all my friends in Kansas. He told me a good

---

[67]The phrase Pell-Mell comes from the French phrase *pesle mesle*, which means to mix. Pell-mell means in a confused or disjointed manner.

deal of news.[68]

November 17th, Thursday
Our Regt. started out on a foraging trip today. Crossed the river at Van Buren and marched out on Frog Bayou and camped. Rained all the afternoon. Got houses to stay in. The 11th U.S. Colored started to Little Rock yesterday. I am on guard tonight.

November 18th, Friday
Marched twelve miles and camped on Little Mulberry. Very muddy marching. No one living in this part of the country. All the houses we pass are deserted.

November 19th, Saturday
Marched twelve miles again today and camped within six miles of Ozark. Showery all day. Got to a potatoe patch tonight, and we soon made for them using our bayonets in lieu of a hoe.

November 20th, Sunday
Marched into Ozark this morning. The advance was fired on by bushwhackers as they came into town. A large train of Rebels were camped four miles from town up on the river. A detachment sent up there. They killed one Rebel. The others took to the brush. The outfit, most of it, came from Missouri and are going to Texas, but the river is so high that they cannot get across now, and were waiting for the river to fall. A squad of bushwhackers were watching or guarding them. They are mostly women and children with the train going to Dixie. The detachment reached and took away from them all goods or articles of northern manufacture or properly called "contraband" goods. We staid in Ozark all night. It is on the north bank of the Ark River. A number of houses have been burnt. Pretty cold night.

---

[68]Francis J. Herron was from Iowa and a banker before the war. He entered service as a captain in the First Iowa Infantry. He led troops at Wilson's Creek, Pea Ridge (where he was wounded and captured) and Prairie Grove. He was briefly in charge of the Army of the Frontier after attaining the rank of major general. He participated in the final stages of the Vicksburg Campaign. After the war he practiced law in Louisiana and served as U. S. Marshal. He was awarded the Congressional Medal of Honor in 1893 for his service at Pea Ridge. He died in New York in 1902. Shea, *War in the West*, 81.

The Twelfth Kansas Infantry waiting to be inspected by General Francis Herron on Garrison Avenue in Fort Smith, November 12, 1864.

Photograph courtesy of
Jules Martino

One section of ten-pounder Parrot guns belonging to the Second Kansas Battery waiting for inspection on Garrison Avenue in Fort Smith, November 12, 1864.

Photograph courtesy of
Jules Martino

Gen. James G. Blunt, ca. 1864.

*Photograph Courtesy of
Butler Center for Arkansas Studies,
Central Arkansas Library System*

November 21ˢᵗ, Monday
Marched ten miles down the river to a mill and camped. Very rough today among the hills. The Cavalry scouts with us killed three bushwhackers. They were dodging around through the brush, thinking to avoid the Inf. Command when these scouts ran on to the chaps. They started to run, but got shot for their pains.

November 22, Tuesday
The mill where we camped is run by horse power. As rations are scarce, we put mules on to run it and ground corn nearly all night. The Col. searched the train last night for stolen property. Arrested several of the boys and teamster and gave some pretty strict orders. Started at 2 p.m. and marched four miles on our return. Nearly all the wagons loaded with corn. Camped on Wm. Howell's place. He was killed yesterday. Was bushwhackers. Awful cold last night.

November 23ʳᵈ, Wednesday
Marched fourteen miles. Passed through Ozark and camped on the Little Rock road, five miles from Ozark. Two more bushwhackers killed this morning, as we came into Ozark. They ran out and the Cav. gave chase and caught them not over a half a mile off, going up on the mountain. We got plenty of fresh pork, and find a potatoe patch occasionally.

November 24ᵗʰ, Thursday
Seven mountaineers came into camp last night and are going to Fort Smith with us. They have lived out in the mountains for several months. Marched fifteen miles and camped on Little Mulberry. Ten Rebels were captured today.

November 25ᵗʰ, Friday
Marched sixteen miles and camped two miles from Van Buren.

November 26ᵗʰ, Saturday
Got into town at sunrise and to Fort Smith at ten a.m. Heard that John Harrbin was killed a few days since by Rebels, while coming from Fort Scott. Sent one dollar to New York City for a book. First Arkansas started to Gibson. The one hundred separtive Rebels, or whatever you choose to call them, went with the First. These fellows say Price, when he was in Missouri, conscripted them, and when he was crossing the Ark River, they left him, it

being the first opportunity they had of leaving. But I doubt their being conscripted. Guess most of them joined of their own will.[69]

December 1st, Thursday

Nothing worthy of note, only that rations are very scarce, barely enough to live on. Duty very heavy – on guard every other day. Getting the time of year for cold weather and we get a little cold weather very frequently. Our winter quarters are very comfortable. There are from four to eight in a cabin. Sherman's progress through Rebeldom is hailed with delight.

December 10th, Saturday

Our Regt. started on a foraging trip to Cave Hill, crossed the river and marched out four miles from the ferry landing and camped for the night. Lt. Col. Waugh of the 2nd Arkansas Infty. in command.[70]

December 11th, Sunday

Passed through Dripping Springs and went on north. Twenty miles from Fort Smith a messenger overtook us from Gen. Thayer, and we were ordered back to Van Buren. Stopped at Dripping Springs and got dinner. This place took its name from the springs that drip down over a ledge of rock. Arrived at Van Buren at sundown, having marched twenty-five miles. This is the coldest day of the winter.

December 12th, Monday

The cause of us being ordered back, is that a boat coming up from Little Rock ran on a snag and sank, below Clarksville somewhere, and the train has to go down and bring up the freight. Our Regt. has to escort the train. Marched out to Frog Bayou, eight miles and camped. Very cold.

December 13th, Tuesday

Marched twelve miles and camped on Little Mulberry. A train of eighty, just from Fort Scott, came up with us, escorted by the 1st Kansas Colored. All are going to the boat. I learned this evening that the boat has been there over

---

[69] John Harbin was from Fort Lincoln, Kansas, and joined the regiment August 16, 1862. He was killed in action November 19, 1864. *Report of the Adjutant General*, 443.

[70] Gideon M. Waugh was lieutenant colonel of the Second Arkansas Infantry (Union).

three weeks. Dispatches were started three different times but all failed to get through. They say a woman on horseback tried and succeeded in getting through. Rode day and night and made the trip in two days.

December 14th, Wednesday
Marched twenty miles and camped opposite Ozark. Our Co. sent out foraging. Went off from the road eight or ten miles and did not get to camp till late at night. Got plenty of forage, also chickens, honey, potatoes and fresh pork. You bet we lived splendid. Have everything our hearts could wish for.

December 15th, Thursday
Marched twelve miles and camped on Horse Head. I went out foraging again. Found plenty, but not as great as yesterday. Camped in cotton house. Rained hard.

December 16th, Friday
Marched fifteen miles today and camped four miles beyond Clarksville. A dispatch bearer supposed to have been killed near Clarksville yesterday, as he was captured by some Rebs. Lt. Cook sent out with a detachment to try and find and bury him. But was unsuccessful. The rear guard saw several squads of bushwhackers. Fired on them several times. We passed a grave today of one of the 2nd Ark. Cav. who was killed by bushwhackers. His body was scarcely covered, head and feet in sight.

December 17th, Saturday
Marched fifteen miles and got to Strathorns' landing, where the boats are. The J. H. Done ran on a log and broke in two pieces. The freight nearly all was saved as the water was very shallow. There are also three other boats here, the water being so low that they can neither get up or down. Two or three Regts. or parts of Regts. are here guarding them. Bushwhackers are very thick through the country now.[71]

December 18th, Sunday
Rained hard all day. Train loading to go to Fort Smith. The Cavalry started back to Lewisburgh this morning. We moved down into the quarters they

---

[71] The *J. H. Done* was a 211-ton stern-wheeler built in 1854 in Shousetown, Pennsylvania. The boat was in the service of the United States Quartermaster Department. Way, *Way's Packet Directory*, 231.

built. These troops have been here three weeks. We hear that Major Gen. Reynolds has superceded Gen. Steele to the command of the Depts. of Arkansas. Rained the hardest kind all day. Guess twill soon raise the river so that the boats can get out of this. Hope it will for, if not, our Regt. has to stay and guard these boats until the train can go to For Smith and return for the remainder.[72]

December 19th, Monday
Still raining very hard. River raising very fast. Think that we will get to go with the train, as the boats can nearly run down the river now.

December 20th, Tuesday
The boats started down the river at nine this morning. Command and train started for Smith. Marched out seven miles and camped by an old mill near Piney. Roads very bad. Has been so much rain. All the small streams very high. Plenty of pine timber in this part of the country. The train is loaded with oats. It seems to me that when provision is as scarce as at Fort Smith that they ought to take grub and nothing but grub.

December 21st, Wednesday
Had to lay out today on account of high water in Piney, cannot cross it. Went out ten miles after forage. Got a large supply of provisions of all kinds. The 1st Colored went in for stealing everything they could find. When they came to camp were all arrested and searched. Had a wagon load of plunder apiece, women's and children's clothes & etc. Several of them arrested. Snowed last night.

December 22nd, Thursday
Piney so high that we cannot cross today. Another detail sent out after forage. Some of the roughest country I have seen for many a day out in the neighborhood of Dover. Some of the boys went out and found a cave, two or three of them near the mouth of piney, filled with clothing, bedding and the like, that the people had laid out. Weaver found one coming down on the Horse Head full of clothes, nearly everything in it, seven boxes full. Col.

---

[72] Joseph J. Reynolds was a native of Kentucky and graduated from West Point in 1843. He fought in Virginia early in the war, and led troops at Tullahoma and Chickamauga. He served in the army after the war until he was court-martialed in 1876, following the Powder River Campaign. Sifakis, *Who Was Who in the Union*, 332.

Waugh searched the whole command tonight for articles taken. Found lots in the train.

December 23rd, Friday
Crossed Piney this morning. The Infantry got into the wagons and crossed. Marched thirteen miles and camped at Clarksville. Four Rebs killed.

December 24th, Saturday
Marched fifteen miles and camped in an old field. Wet and rainy all day. Some of the boys went off the road and killed one Reb and wounded two others, burned a house that harbored them.

December 25th, Sunday
Christmas
Marched fifteen miles and camped three miles from Big Mulberry. Some of the boys went out in the mountains on the north side of the road and got lost. Did not get to camp till after night. A squad of bushwhackers ran on to the command today. The whole darky Regt. fired on them.

December 26th, Monday
Marched eighteen miles and camped on Frog Bayou. After supper a dispatch came ordering us to Van Buren tonight. Were all very tired with the day's march, but had to go on. Started at dark. Got to Van Buren at 11 p.m., and laid out in the streets –anywhere till morning.

December 27th, Tuesday
Crossed over to Fort Smith today. Are preparing to evacuate Fort Smith. Four boats loaded with Hospital outfit and artillery started down the river today. Received four letters.

December 28th, Wednesday
The 3rd Brigade Cav. started down the river today. One year ago today we arrived at Fort Smith.

Nothing more of interest occurred during the month of December.

1865

January 1st, 1865, Sunday

I am on picket guard today on the road to Rector farm. Twenty Rebels were at the Rector house. We could see them from the picket post. Some of them came down within a quarter of a mile of us. Are still preparing to leave this place. A great many of the citizens are building flatboats to go down to Little Rock on. On the 5th, two of the 18th Iowa killed by bushwhackers out beyond the picket. Ben Parks came down from Fort Scott. 9th was ordered to start to Little Rock this morning, but is countermandering the one to evacuate Fort Smith. Three boats came up with commissaries, and this post is to be held as a military post. Bushwhackers are very bold. Have a great deal of duty to do. Boats to unload. The Infty. has all the guarding to do. No Cav. here.[73]

---

[73] Elias Rector owned the Rector farm. Born in Virginia, he came to Arkansas in 1825. President Andrew Jackson appointed him U.S. Marshal for the Western District of Arkansas, a post he held for sixteen years under four presidents. He was also appointed Superintendent of Southwestern Indian Affairs, and in this capacity he directly oversaw the removal of Billy Bowlegs and the remaining Seminoles in Florida. Rector owned a large, prosperous plantation in what is now the north side of Fort Smith, Arkansas. His cousin Henry M. Rector was the sixth governor of Arkansas and led the state through secession. Rector's brother-in-law was Benjamin DuVal, a Confederate officer. Rector's daughter married General William Cabell of the Confederate Army. Opposed to secession but sympathetic to the South, Rector and his family remained in Fort Smith until 1862, then went to Texas as the war spread to western Arkansas. The family returned in 1866 to find their farm and possessions confiscated by federal authorities. "Kate Rector Diary," *The Journal* 1 (December 1977): 58-66.

January 19th, Thursday

Three boats left for Little Rock today, and just below Ozark were fired on by Brooks' command. He had one piece of artillery. The Chippewa was burned. The Annie Jacobs had eleven cannonballs hit her. She was run out on a sand bar on the north side of the river and saved from being burned. The soldiers on the Chippewa were taken off prisoners. A lot of refugees, women and children, on the boat got frightened when they fired on the boat and jumped overboard and were drowned. Hiram Rhoton returned from Fort Scott. He has been home on furlough. Started to come down with the train that was captured last Sept. by Gano. He got a horse and went back to Fort Scott when the train surrendered. So escaped from them. John Parks of our Co., who was captured last fall, when the 11th Colored was attacked.[74]

Nothing of importance more occurred during the month. A great deal of wet weather, some intolerable cold weather. I have been sick for the three weeks past. The river is and has been all this month good for boating. Consequently boats have been running pretty regular. Are bringing considerable grub. A great deal of duty to do –guard and fatigue.

---

[74] William H. Brooks was from Michigan but fought gallantly for the Confederacy at Wilson's Creek, Pea Ridge, Prairie Grove, Helena and Jenkins' Ferry. He led the Thirty-fourth Arkansas Infantry and a guerilla brigade during the war. The official report of the action follows:

Order of Maj. Gen. John B. Magruder, C. S. Army, commanding District of Arkansas, of operations January 14-17.

GENERAL ORDERS, No. 18., HEADQUARTERS DISTRICT OF ARKANSAS, Washington, January 25, 1865.

The major-general commanding takes pleasure in announcing to the army that Col. Brooks, commanding Brooks' brigade, composed of Brooks' men proper, Newton's regiment, and Stirman's battalion, after a long and difficult march to the Arkansas River, attacked a heavier force of the enemy near Dardanelle, drove him into his works, killing 8, wounding 19, and capturing 2; loss on our side, 1 killed and 15 wounded. Col. Brooks, hearing of the approach of steamers from above, by a forced march, with 400 men, reached the proper point at sunrise on the 16th instant. Having placed a piece of artillery and his men in ambush, at 1 o'clock on the 17th, he permitted the leading boat to come well in range, when he opened upon her with his infantry and this piece. She was raked from stem to stern and soon surrendered. She proved to be the New Chippewa. The prisoners consist of 1 officer and 29 men of the Fiftieth Indiana and 40 negroes;

February 1ˢᵗ, Wednesday

Nothing of interest occurred for several days. Have a great deal of cold wet weather. I am able for duty again. Boats running very regular. On Sunday evening the 12ᵗʰ, the Steamer Annie Jacobs arrived having Gen. Bussy and Staff. He comes to take command of this Division in Gen. Thayer's stead.[75]

---

also the captain, crew, and a large number of refugee families from Fort Smith. After removing everything valuable the boat was fired. The steamer *Annie Jacobs* next hove in sight. She was immediately attacked, and the fire was returned by the troops on board. She attempted to destroy our artillerists; our artillery, however, soon disabled her, and she grounded upon an island. Here many men [were] drowned in attempting to make their escape to the opposite bank. During the engagement with the Jacobs the Lotus came down. The troops on board were driven into the water and she to the north bank of the river, where most of them escaped, the iron axle of one piece of artillery having broken. Finding the boats too distant for an effective fire of musketry, Col. Brooks returned to his camps, taking with him 82 prisoners and the refugee families captured. Federal casualties, 27 killed and wounded, besides those who were drowned; our own loss, 1 killed and 15 wounded. A large quantity of the enemy's store were destroyed.

Col.'s Newton and Stirman and Lieut. Lockhart are spoken of in high terms by Col. Brooks in his report of their operations. Information has also been received from Maj. Gen. M M Parsons that Capt. Webb, who was ordered to destroy the enemy's mills at Pine Bluff and to rid the country of graybacks, has succeeded in capturing one company, thirty-seven strong, a number of horses, arms, &c. The commanding general takes great pleasure in returning his thanks to both officers and men of the several commands for their gallant conduct on this occasion.

By command of Maj. Gen. J. B. Magruder:

EDMUND P. TURNER,
Assistant Adjutant-Gen.

OR, vol. 48, pt. 2, 16-17.

Hiram Rhoton was from Turkey Creek, Kansas, and enlisted August 16, 1862. He mustered out June 30, 1865. *Report of the Adjutant General,* 443.

The *Annie Jacobs* was a 148-ton stern-wheeler built at Mound City, Illinois, in 1863. In 1864 the United States Quartermaster Department enlisted the boat into service. Way, *Way's Packet Directory,* 24.

[75] Cyrus Bussey was from Ohio and became a politician in Iowa before the war. As colonel of the Third Iowa Cavalry he fought at Pea Ridge. He later fought at Arkansas Post and Vicksburg before attaining the rank of general. He served out the rest of the

February 13th, Monday

The Steamer Virginia Barton come up today. Had on fifteen hundred barrels of flour, besides a large quantity of other freight. Had on board the 22nd Ohio veterans. Our Regt. unloaded the boat. Gen. Thayer and Staff left for Little Rock on the 16th. Capt. Bunn resigned and started home on the 19th. Sent some letters by him. A train came up from Little Rock.[76]

February 22nd, Wednesday

The Carrie Jacobs came up. Had on board more troops. Our Regt. to go down on her. All of the Kansas troops are to go to Little Rock and other troops come, in our place. Am pleased to get away from here, as I have staid in this place long enough.[77]

February 23rd, Thursday

The Virginia Barton started to Gibson this morning. Our Regt. left camp at noon. Marched down to the river. Only five companies could get aboard. The others have to wait for the next boat. Rose Hambleton came up just as we started. Bade adieu to Fort Smith at three p.m. and went scudding down the Arkansas, band playing patriotic tunes. Left Van Buren at dusk. Co. "K" up on the hurricane deck where we can get plenty of fresh air which is very cooling this February evening. Feels rather wintery. Carrie Jacobs ran all night, at pretty brisk rate. Passed the A D Hine tied up to bank. Had to get up out of a "cold bed" and walk the deck to keep warm – about "frooze out". Got to Dardanelle at daylight. Met the Annie Jacobs here. Kept on. Very wet and windy. The 24th was very windy the fore part of the day. The boat could hardly keep the channel. Got to Lewisburgh at one p.m. Stopped only a few minutes. Missouri troops are stationed here. Got to Little Rock at sundown on Friday the 24th. It's called three hundred miles by water from Fort Smith to Little Rock. I find it a much better way of traveling than by land

---

war in Arkansas and mustered out August 24, 1865. He practiced law after the war until his death in 1915. Sifakis, *Who Was Who in the Union*, 59.

[76] The *Virginia Barton* was a 219-ton side-wheeler built in 1864 in Brownsville, Pennsylvania. The boat was sold to the United States Quartermaster Department in 1864. Way, *Way's Packet Directory*, 472.

[77] The *Carrie Jacobs* was a 156-ton side-wheeler built at Brownsville, Pennsylvania, in 1863. The boat was sold to the United States Quartermaster Department in 1864. *Ibid.*, 73.

and on foot, as we generally do when moving from one place to another.[78]

February 25th, Saturday
Staid on the boat last night. Got an awful wetting. Rained nearly all night, thought it would wash me off the hurricane deck. Left the boat this morning and marched out through town. Went in the quarters of the 40th Iowa, who relieved us at Fort Smith. Have got pretty good quarters, out southwest from town.

February 26th, Sunday
The remainder of the Regiment arrived today on the Rose Hambleton. Went around through town considerable today. Very lively place to what we have been used to at Fort Smith. Cars and boats coming and going all the time. Will not be put on duty for a few days, so as to have time to draw a new outfit of accoutrements.

March 13,
The 13th Kansas have come to this place. 14th Kansas Cavalry gone to Pine Bluffs. 6th Kansas are at Devall's Bluff. Are to be mustered out this month. Our Regt. is assigned to the 1st Brigade, 1st Division, 7th Army Corps. Have been put on guard duty at penitentiary. There are three or four hundred Rebel prisoners in there. Are going to make a garden for the Regt.'s use. Lt. Cook is in charge. It is on the north side of the river, three miles below town. Don't think that twill amount to much. A good many Rebs are coming in and surrendering up. Can get plenty of papers to read at the Christian Commission. So time does not drag so heavily. Had Inspection three times. Must want to see how we look.[79]

---

[78] The *Rose Hambleton* was a 154-ton side-wheeler built in 1861 in Cincinnati, Ohio. *Ibid.*, 402.

The *A.D. Hine* was built in 1860 in Monongahela, Pennsylvania. *Ibid.,* 5.

[79] The Y.M.C.A. organized the United States Christian Commission in New York in 1861. The commission provided paper, pens, and postage to Union soldiers during the war. Christian literature was also distributed in the form of "knapsack" booklets and tracts. Additionally, the U.S.C.C. raised six million dollars for soldier relief and aid. The organization disbanded in 1866. Lemuel Moss, *Annals of the United States Christian Commission* (Philadelphia: J.B. Lippincott & Co., 1868).

April

Was paid on 5th of the month. Have had some of the hardest storms this month that I have seen since in the service – rain all the time. River up full bank. Jackman started home on the 7th. I am on sick furlough. I sent eighty-five dollars home by him. News of the great victories in Virginia received today. Great rejoicing in camp and town. Petersburgh was captured on the 2nd and our Army took possession of Richmond on the 3rd. A national salute was fired on the occasion.[80]

April 11th, Tuesday

Lee's Army surrendered to Lt. Gen. Grant on the 9th. His Army was paroled and allowed to go home and not to take up arms until properly exchanged.

April 12th, Wednesday

A salute of two hundred guns fired in honor of Lee's surrender. All the camp illumined, also the town. Capt Miserez returned from Kansas today.

April 13th, Thurday

Our Regt. had a grand torch light procession this evening. Marched all around town and to Gen. Reynolds' and Saloman's Headquarters. All the town brilliantly illuminated. Our boys had various devices and mottos among which was "The Success of our Cause –The Hope of the World", and "How are you, Maximillian", also a coffin representing Jeff Davis. All passed off very satisfactorily to all. Lee's force that was paroled numbered twenty-three thousand. A large amount of property taken in Petersburgh and Richmond. Mobile also captured.[81]

---

[80] William Jackman was from Turkey Creek, Kansas, and enlisted August 24, 1862. He was promoted to sergeant September 30, 1862. He mustered out June 23, 1865. *Report of the Adjutant General*, 442.

A national salute consisted of firing a round for each state in the Union. In April 1865, there were thirty-five states.

[81] Frederick Saloman was from Prussia. He settled in Wisconsin before the war. He had one brother who was governor of that state and two brothers who were also brigadier generals. He attained the rank of general during the war, fighting at Wilson's Creek, Helena, and, notably, covering Steele's retreat from Jenkins' Ferry in 1864. He was a surveyor after the war and died in 1897. Sifakis, *Who Was Who in the Union*, 351.

April 15th Saturday

Kirby Smith sent in a flag of truce to learn (we suppose) the particulars of Lee's surrender, and that he will do the same. Gen. Reynolds sent back the particulars of the surrender.

April 17th, Monday

The news of President Lincoln's assassination. All the flags at half-mast during the day and a gun fired at every half hour during the day. All the town draped in mourning. All of rejoicing of past few days turned into mourning.

Mobile was captured on the 10th of the month. Andy Johnson was inaugurated on the 15th.

Report that Sherman is getting Joe Johnson in a tight place in North Carolina. I got my picture taken and sent home.

April 28th, Friday

Gen. Blunt arrived here today. Reported that there is an expedition going South, and that he is to command it. Also that the 5th Army Corps is coming here to join in the expedition. Can't say how true tis, but from all appearances judge that something is up. Gen. Reynolds has gone to Fort Smith to review the troops. I received a letter from Capt. Montgomery, also his photograph. Are trying to raise an engineer Regt. from out of the command here. All that have less than ten months to serve can re-enlist for one and two years just as they choose. Are getting one hundred recruits or more from a Regt. I will try a citizen's life awhile, I believe, and see how I like it.[82]

April 29th

The report now is that Blunt is to go to Gibson to take command there, also that he will take troops from this place. The news of Gen. Sherman and Joe Johnston peace treaty reached here today. Is condemned by all. After marching all through the South and knowing no impossibilities to make such

---

[82] On April 8, 1865, Major General John Pope wrote a letter to General Grant outlining a plan to take three columns of troops in Arkansas, one each from Little Rock, Dardanelle and Fort Smith, and march them to Texas. The object would be to push into Texas and Indian Territory and sweep up the remaining Confederate forces and supplies as well as to add much needed forage land for the animals. *OR*, vol. 48, pt. 2, 51-53.

terms as he did, and the Rebel Army in his power, almost.[83]

April 30th, Sunday

This is a warm and pleasant day, the anniversary of the Battle of Jenkins' Ferry. How different our situation today. May the future ever be brighter.

May 1st, Monday

Received the news of J. W. Booth's death, the assassin of the President, also the capture of one of his accomplices. May they all be brought to speedy justice.

May 2nd, Tuesday

Today is the day that President Lincoln's body arrives at his old home at Springfield, Illinois. All the troops were paraded this morning and then no more unnecessary work or business during the day. In the evening, I attended a temperance lecture. Several different speakers addressed the audience. Very good remarks – and some very good advice given.

May 4th, Thursday

Joe Johnstons' Army surrendered to Gen. Sherman on the 25th of April on the same terms that Lee surrendered on . This closes up the war east of the Mississippi – as all the Rebel forces have now surrendered in that part of the country.

The 4th Kansas Cavalry came up from Pine Bluff today –are to go to Ft. Gibson. Getting to be pretty warm weather. Horses for the Cavalry Regts., mules, wagons and ambulances are being shipped here by every boat – suppose they are for the contemplated expedition South. The soldiers in hospitals all over the United States are ordered mustered out immediately. All that do not need any more treatment. All the news shows that a large proportion of the troops will be mustered out. Think our time will come soon.[84]

---

[83] Strong echoes the feelings of many who felt the surrender treaties were too generous to the Rebels.

[84] GENERAL ORDERS, No. 77. WAR DEPT, ADJUTANT-GEN.'S OFFICE, Washington, D. C., April 28, 1865.
For reducing expenses of the military establishment.

Jeff Davis was captured on the 11th, just near Irwinville, Georgia. The southern Confederacy is "played out" now. All that remains is to take in Kirby Smith. A flag of truce came in from Kirby Smith today (Sunday, 14th). Have not heard whether business. All the peace negotiations with Kirby Smith as yet have failed. The weather is very warm almost unendurable. Measures are being taken to reduce the Army. Are hoping to get discharged.

May 23rd, Tuesday
Lt. Barrett has resigned. Started home today. Have to drill every day when not on duty. Pretty hard this warm weather. Hope that it will soon play out.

May 24th, Wednesday
Fifty Rebels came up on the Steamer Geneva today – are from Shreveport. They left on the 16th. Say that Kirby Smith surrendered the day they left. If so, the rebellion is gone up, in my opinion, in a hurry.[85]

May 25th, Thursday
Received my book today. Another lot of Rebels came in today. Quite a train with them. Some prominent Rebels that left here and went South to secure their "rights" are returning. Rebels have continued to come in the

---

Ordered:

VI. All officers and enlisted men who have been prisoners of war, and now on furlough or at the parole camps, and all recruits in rendezvous, except those for the Regular Army, and the First Army Corps (Hancock's) will likewise be honorably discharged. Officers whose duty it is under the regulations of the service to make out rolls and other final papers connected with the discharge and payment of soldiers are directed to make them out without delay, so that this order may be carried into effect immediately. Cmdg. generals of armies and departments will look to the prompt execution of this work.

By order of the Secretary of War:
W. A. NICHOLS,
 Assistant Adjutant-Gen.
OR, vol. 48, pt. 2, 397.

This order was applied to those in hospitals not requiring further care as well.

[85] The *Geneva* was a 127-ton side-wheeler built in 1863 in Brownsville, Pennsylvania. Way, *Way's Packet Directory*, 184.

whole week – averaging fifty per day. Some of these came from Dick Taylor's army east of the Mississippi. Others from Shreveport and say that the Rebels are all disbanding.[86]

May 27th, Saturday
Three of the Company, Beltes, Ellis, and Morse were mustered out at the hospital today. Will start home as soon as they are paid. We still have to drill every day. Seems to me as very foolish as there but little attention paid to it –as the boys all think it an imposition on them. Hasten the day that we are all mustered out.

June 1st, Thursday
Very warm weather. Rebels coming at the rate of two or three hundred per day. Some with horses, arms and equipment –others without. Say they left them at Shreveport or Washington. Most of them as soon as they get their papers and paroles, start for their homes. Live mostly in this state and Missouri. Went down to Regimental farm yesterday. Came back today. Got a couple of fine fish. The mustering out question is the all absorbing topic now. Ellis & Beltes started home yesterday. Quite a number of the Regt. have been mustered out that were in the hospital. Drill has been coutermanded. All of the 9th Wisconsin Infty whose time of Service expires prior to next October are mustered out. The remainder of the Regt. left on the 3rd for Camden – going down the Ark River. A Cavalry expedition has also started for Camden. Rebels continue to come in at the rate of four or five hundred per day.[87]

June 8th, Thursday
There was a grand review of the 1st Brigade today by Gen. Reynolds, Saloman and Clayton. Col. Adams resigned and left today. The 12th Michigan Vet.

---

[86] Richard Taylor was the son of Zachary Taylor and brother of the first wife of Jefferson Davis. He was born in Kentucky in 1826. Taylor spent his early life at various frontier posts including Fort Smith, Arkansas. He attended Harvard and Yale, served as his father's secretary during the Mexican War, and operated a sugar plantation in Louisiana before the war. He served the Confederate Army as a brigadier general at Manassas, Jackson's Valley Campaign, and later served in the Trans-Mississippi. He was the last officer to surrender east of the Mississippi River in May 1865. After the war he lobbied for leniency for former Confederates to President Andrew Johnson.

[87] Albert Ellis was from Mound City, Kansas, and enlisted August 20, 1862. He mustered out May 26, 1865. *Report of the Adjutant General*, 443.

Vols. arrived today –think we will get away from here in a few days.[88]

June 9th, Friday

Major Kennedy returned today from Kansas.

June 10th, Saturday

Had another Grand Review this morning at five o'clock. All of the Division were out. Number out estimated at ten thousand.

June 11th, Sunday

9th Iowa Cavalry Veterans arrived today. Some of the troops are to leave in a day or two.

June 12th, Monday

Col. Adams has been ordered back to the Regiment to take command. Had another Grand Review today. More troops out than on Saturday and more Regiments in our Brigade.

June 13th, Tuesday

The 12th Michigan Infantry started to Washington today, and to be stationed in that place. This Regt. numbers thirteen hundred men, the largest Infantry Regt. I have seen since in the service. The 9th Iowa Cav. started to Lewisburg also today. Rained considerable.

Have commenced mustering out troops. The 1st Mo. Cav. were mustered out today. Are mustering out some Artillery Cos. too. The Rebels still continue to come in. They report everyone is south of here.

June 22nd, Thursday

Received orders to send in rolls as soon as they could be made to be mustered out on them. All detached Service men in this Dept. are relieved from duty – or rather those that belong to 11th and 13th Kansas and 35th Mo. One of our Colored Co. on guard last night (J. Archey) killed one of the 13th Kansas

---

[88] Powell Clayton was a native of Pennsylvania. He moved to Kansas in the 1850s and worked as a civil engineer. He fought at Wilson's Creek as a captain in the First Kansas Infantry and was later promoted lieutenant colonel, colonel and brigadier general. He was governor of Arkansas from 1868 through 1871. His brother, William, was District Attorney for Judge Isaac C. Parker in Fort Smith after the war.

who was a prisoner and ran off or started to, from him. Are having very hot weather. Have been unfit for duty for several days on account of a swelling on my hand.[89]

June 25th, Sunday

Peter Eby died this morning at half past six o'clock –was taken to the Hospital only yesterday and out of his right mind nearly all the time, the poor fellow wanted to go home so bad.

Our Regt. was relieved from duty this morning. All of the rolls are made out –think we will leave shortly.

June 26th, Monday

The 13th Kansas Infantry were mustered out of the Service today. Are expecting to be mustered out of the Service soon. Had a long rambel after blackberries. There is an abundance of them here in the woods.

June 27th, Wednesday

The 35th Missouri was mustered out today. A Mo. Cavalry Regt. started for Missouri today. Nothing more of importance occurred during the two days following.

June 30th, Friday

The long looked for day has at last arrived. We were mustered out today at one o'clock. Don't know how soon we will start home. We are to be paid off at Lawrence and get our final discharge. The recruits are to be kept in the Service. There is about one hundred in the Regt. Capt. Jennings of "E" Co. is to be Capt. Lt. J. Berkshire of "I" Co. and Cook of Co. "K" are their Lieutenants.[90]

---

[89] Jonathan Archey was from Twin Springs, Kansas, and enlisted September 9, 1862. He mustered out with the regiment June 30, 1865. *Report of the Adjutant General*, 442.

Henry Fowles was from Atchison County, Kansas, and enlisted in Co. D, Thirteenth Kansas Cavalry on September 4, 1862. He died in Little Rock, Arkansas, on June 22, 1865, of wounds received while attempting to escape from the guardhouse. *Ibid.*, 454.

[90] A. Jackson Jennings was from Eudora, Kansas, and was commissioned first lieutenant, Co. E, September 26, 1862. He was promoted captain January 16, 1864, and

Lt. James Berkshire, Twelfth Kansas, Co. I, ca. 1864.

Photograph courtesy of
The Kansas State Historical Society

The steamboat *Rowena* docked at Memphis, ca. 1863.
Photograph courtesy Huddleston Collection, UALR Archives & Special Collections

July 1ˢᵗ, Saturday

The 13ᵗʰ Kansas started for home today. We are expecting to get off in a few days. Weather is getting to be very warm. I am anxious to get away for fear that t'will be sickly soon.

July 3ʳᵈ, Monday

The 35ᵗʰ Mo. Started for home this morning. An order was received to muster out all the recruits in the Regt., a more pleased set of fellows I never saw. They were mustered out this evening. Regt. left camp at six this p.m. and marched over to the depot. Are to leave at seven o'clock tomorrow morning. The 7ᵗʰ Div. of the 16ᵗʰ Corps are at Devalls Bluff coming here. One Regt. arrived tonight

July 4ᵗʰ, Tuesday

The morning was ushered in by a National Salute from the different batteries in the Hurrah for the glorious fourth of July, the anniversary of the Independence of the greatest Republic on this globe. Left on the cars at seven o'clock a.m. Passed a train at Brownsville station with Regt. going to Little Rock. Saw some of the most beautiful prairies I ever saw. It made me feel like getting out of the wilderness. Arrived at Bluffs at eleven a.m. Got on board the Steamer Melnotte. Duvall's Bluffs is a little one horse town railroad station on White River. Left at twelve p.m. White River is a narrow crooked stream but very deep. Our boat had some difficulty in making the short turns, turned around several times. Sometime hardly manageable. The banks of this stream are very low bordered on both sides by cypress swamps. Passed two or three little towns during the day, but they are all deserted. I was a dead man in a bunch of drift this evening. At dark the boat tied up for the night six miles above St. Charles. Sixty miles below the Bluffs. During the night the Rowena passed down.[91]

---

mustered out with the regiment June 30, 1865. *Report of the Adjutant General*, 430.

James Berkshire was from Spring Hill, Kansas, and enlisted in Co. I August 25, 1862. He was promoted sergeant September 30, 1862. He was then promoted second lieutenant September 15, 1863. Finally, he was promoted first lieutenant August 13, 1864. He mustered out June 30, 1865. *Ibid.*, 440.

[91] The national salute consisted of thirty-six guns honoring the newly admitted state of Nevada.

The *Melnotte* was a stern-wheel packet built in 1856 in California, Pennsylvania. Way,

July 5ᵗʰ, Wednesday
Started at daylight. Met the <u>Cleona.</u> Had some trouble and delay in getting around some of the bends. Arrived at the mouth of White River and steamed out in the broad Mississippi River at twelve o'clock M. Landed at White River landing at the mouth of the White River and took on a supply of coal. Left the mouth of the White River at four this p.m. and started up the "Father of Waters". The old steamer <u>Melnotte</u> proved beyond a doubt that she is a fast boat –ran all night. Met quite a number of steamers.[92]

July 6ᵗʰ, Thursday
Arrived at Helena at sunrise – eighty three miles above White River. Stopped and took on some coal. Here is where Price attacked our forces on the 4ᵗʰ of July, 1862 [1863], and got handsomely whipped. Have fair weather and cooling breezes, so we keep quite comfortable. Met quite a number of boats during the day. Arrived Memphis at eight o'clock p.m. Staid all night. This is one hundred and seventy five miles above the mouth of White River.

July 7ᵗʰ, Friday
Changed boats. Got aboard the large sidewheel packet, <u>City of Cairo.</u> Staid in the City nearly all day. Memphis is a pretty city on a high bluff, a place of considerable importance. Left at five p.m. and went on up the river. The City of Cairo makes about twice the speed the old <u>Melnotte</u> did. The plantations are not much, abandoned generally as lower down the river.[93]

July 8ᵗʰ, Saturday
Passed the boat with the 35ᵗʰ Mo. on board during the night. Also passed Fort Pillow, where Forrest massacred our Colored Soldiers. During the day passed several mail stations and towns. The principal one New Madrid, Mo., Hickman and Columbus, Ky. Passed Island No. Ten about noon.

Way's Packet Directory, 318.

The *Rowena* was a 341-ton side-wheeler built in 1864 in Cincinnati, Ohio. *Ibid.*, 403.

[92]The *Cleona* was a stern-wheel packet built in 1864 in Cincinnati, Ohio. *Ibid.*, 100.

[93] The *City of Cairo* was a side-wheel packet built in 1864 in Metropolis, Illinois. *Ibid.*, 89.

Arrived at Cairo at dusk at the mouth of Ohio River. Saw gunboats and Monitors run all night.[94]

July 9th, Sunday
Run all day. Met a large number of steamboats during the day. There's none that can pass the City of Cairo. Passed Cape Girardeau, Chester, St. Marys and St. Genevieve. Are pretty towns situated on the bluffs. There are high bluffs on both sides of the river nearly all the way. Quite different from the lower Mississippi. Had two very heavy storms of wind and rain. Tied up the boat during the first one.

July 10th, Monday
Arrived at St. Louis at 12 o'clock last night. Staid here until four this p.m., then took the North Missouri Railroad and traveled all night. Arrived at Macon City on the Hannibal & St. Joe Road at noon today.

July 11th, Tuesday
Changed cars here on the H. and St. Joe Road and run all night. The Regt. on two trains. This is the roughest road I ever saw.

July 12, Wednesday
Arrived at St. Joe at five this morning. Staid over until noon, then took the train for Weston. Arrived there at half past two p.m. Then got aboard the steamer M. S. Mepham and went to Wyandotte. Met the 13th Kansas between Leavenworth and Wyandotte. They had four days start on us and we beat them to Leavenworth. Arrived at Wyandotte at dusk and staid all night.[95]

July 13th, Thursday
Took the cars at 7 this morning and arrived at Lawrence at 11 o'clock. Went

---

[94]Fort Pillow was on the Mississippi River and named for Mexican War hero Gideon Pillow. Federal forces took the Confederate fort in June of 1862. In April of 1864, Confederate General Nathan Bedford Forrest attacked the Federal garrison there and was accused of the massacre of black troops. Controversy remains today concerning Forrest's actions. Jack Hurst, *Nathan Bedford Forrest: A Biography* (New York: A.A. Knopf, 1993).

[95] The *M.S. Mepham* was a 683-ton side-wheeler built in 1864 in Elizabeth, Pennsylvania. Way, *Way's Packet Directory*, 300.

into camp on the north side of the Kansas River.

July 15th, Saturday
The citizens gave us a grand reception. Had a splendid dinner and speeches. Then received our discharge papers and turned in our guns and equipment. The 2nd and 14th Kansas Cavalry arrived today. I staid at Mr. Wag's part of the time.

July 17, Monday
Signed the Pay Rolls today. Spent the day in rambling around through town.

July 18th, Tuesday
Commenced paying the Regt. today and bothered along until the 20th before our Co. got paid. Rained every day. Very muddy.

~End of Diary~

Henry A. Strong, ca. 1890.

*Photograph courtesy of
Carolyn Gleason and Ralph Moody*

BIBLIOGRAPHY

Abel, Annie Heloise. *The American Indian as Participant in the Civil War*. Cleveland: The Arthur H. Clark Co., 1919.

_____. *The American Indian as Slaveholder and Secessionist*. St. Clair Shores, MI: Scholarly Press, 1972.

Arms and Equipment of the Confederacy. Alexandria, VA: Time-Life Books, 1991.

Arms and Equipment of the Union. Alexandria, VA: Time-Life Books, 1991.

Bearss, Edwin C. *Steele's Retreat from Camden and the Battle of Jenkins' Ferry*. Little Rock: Arkansas Civil War Centennial Commission, 1967.

_____. "Federal Generals Squabble Over Fort Smith, 1863-1864." *Arkansas Historical Quarterly* 29 (Summer 1970): 119-151.

_____. *The Battle of Wilson's Creek*. Diamond, MO: George Washington Carver Birthplace District Association, 1975.

Bearss, Edwin C. and Arrell M. Gibson. *Fort Smith: Little Gibraltar on the Arkansas*. Norman: University of Oklahoma Press, 1969.

Britton, Wiley. *The Civil War on the Border*. 2 vols. New York: G.P. Putnam, 1891–1904.

_____. *Memoirs of the Rebellion on the Border, 1863*. Lincoln: University of Nebraska Press, 1993.

_____. *The Union Indian Brigade in the Civil War*. Ottawa, KS: Kansas Heritage Press, 1994.

Castel, Albert E. *General Sterling Price and the Civil War in the West*. Baton Rouge: Louisiana State University Press, 1968.

_____. *A Frontier State at War: Kansas, 1861-1865*. Westport, CT:

Greenwood Press, 1979.

_____. *Civil War Kansas: Reaping the Whirlwind.* Lawrence: University Press of Kansas, 1997.

_____. *William Clarke Quantrill: His Life and Times.* Norman: University of Oklahoma Press, 1999.

Christ, Mark K. *Rugged and Sublime: The Civil War in Arkansas.* Fayetteville: University of Arkansas Press, 1994.

Cornish, Dudley Taylor. *The Sable Arm: Black Troops in the Union Army, 1861-1865.* Lawrence: University of Kansas Press, 1987.

Cowper, William. *The Diverting History of John Gilpin.* New York: E.P. Dutton, 1899.

Cox, Steve. *"The Action on Massard Prairie." The Journal* 4 (April 1980): 11-13.

Crawford, Samuel Johnson. *Kansas in the Sixties.* Chicago: A.C. McClurg & Co., 1911.

Cunningham, Frank. *General Stand Watie's Confederate Indians.* San Antonio: Naylor Co., 1959.

Dale, Edward Everett, and Gaston Litton. *Cherokee Cavaliers Forty Years of Cherokee History as Told in the Correspondence of the Ridge-Watie-Boudinot Family.* Norman: University of Oklahoma Press, 1995.

Dyer, Frederick H. *A Compendium of the War of the Rebellion.* Des Moines, IA: The Dyer Publishing Co., 1908.

Faulk, Odie B., Kenny Arthur Franks, and Paul F. Lambert. *Early Military Forts and Posts in Oklahoma.* Oklahoma City: Oklahoma Historical Society, 1978.

Foner, Jack D. *Blacks and the Military in American History: A New Perspective.* New York: Praeger, 1974.

Franks, Kenny Arthur. *Stand Watie and the Agony of the Cherokee Nation.* Memphis: Memphis State University Press, 1979.

Furry, William, ed. *The Preacher's Tale: The Civil War Journal of Rev. Francis Springer, Chaplain, U.S. Army of the Frontier.* Fayetteville: University of Arkansas Press, 2001.

Gaines, W. Craig. *The Confederate Cherokees: John Drew's Regiment of Mounted Rifles.* Baton Rouge: Louisiana State University Press, 1989.

Gladstone, William A. *Men of Color.* Gettysburg, PA: Thomas Publications, 1993.

Glatthaar, Joseph T. *Forged in Battle: The Civil War Alliance of Black Soldiers and White Officers.* New York: Free Press, 1990.

Goodrich, Thomas. *Black Flag: Guerilla Warfare on the Western Border, 1861-1865*. Bloomington: Indiana University Press, 1995.

Grayson, G.W., and W. David Baird. *A Creek Warrior for the Confederacy: The Autobiography of Chief G.W. Grayson*. Norman: University of Oklahoma Press, 1988.

Greene, John W. *Camp Ford Prison and How I Escaped: An Incident of the Civil War*. Toledo, OH: Greene, 1893.

Hargrove, Hondon B. *Black Union Soldiers in the Civil War*. Jefferson, NC: McFarland & Co., 1988.

Harrington, Fred Harvey. *Fighting Politican: Major General N.P. Banks*. Philadelphia: University of Pennsylvania Press, 1948.

Hauptman, Laurence M. *Between Two Fires: American Indians in the Civil War*. New York: Free Press, 1996.

Heidler, David Stephen, Jeanne T. Heidler, and David J. Coles. *Encyclopedia of the American Civil War: A Political, Social, and Military History*. Santa Barbara, CA: ABC-CLIO, 2000.

Hurst, Jack. *Nathan Bedford Forrest: A Biography*. New York: A.A. Knopf, 1993.

Josephy, Alvin M. *The Civil War in the American West*. New York: A.A. Knopf, 1991.

Kansas. *Report of the Adjutant General of the State of Kansas, 1861-'65*. Vol. I. Topeka: Kansas State Print Co., 1896.

"Kate Rector Diary." *The Journal* 1 (December 1977): 58-66.

Knight, Wilfred. *Red Fox: Stand Watie and the Confederate Indian Nations During the Civil War Years in Indian Territory*. Glendale, CA: Arthur H. Clark Co., 1988.

Lindberg, Kip. Telephone interview with editor, 2001.

Monaghan, Jan. *Civil War on the Western Border, 1854-1865*. Boston: Little, Brown and Co., 1955.

Moss, Lemuel. *Annals of the United States Christian Commission*. Philadelphia: J.B. Lippincott & Co., 1868.

Nalty, Bernard C. *Strength for the Fight: A History of Black Americans in the Military.* New York: Free Press, 1986.

"Northern Troops in Fort Smith, 1863." *The Journal* 5 (April 1981): 27-33.

Oates, Stephen B. *Confederate Cavalry West of the River*. Austin: University of Texas Press, 1961.

Perdue, Theda. *Slavery and the Evolution of the Cherokee Society, 1540-1866*. Knoxville: University of Tennessee Press, 1979.

Pollan, Carolyn. "Fort Smith Under Union Rule: September 1, 1863-Fall,

1865." *The Journal* 6 (April 1982): 24-28.

Purvis, Doris. *A Little History About Mound City, Kansas and Our Neighbors*. Mound City, KS: Mound City Historical Society, 1976.

Quarles, Benjamin. *The Negro in the Civil War*. Boston: Little, Brown and Co., 1953.

Shea, William L., and Earl J. Hess. *Pea Ridge: Civil War Campaign in the West*. Chapel Hill: University of North Carolina Press, 1992.

Shea, William L. *War in the West: Pea Ridge and Prairie Grove*. Abilene, TX: McWhiney Foundation Press, 1998.

Sifakis, Stewart. *Who Was Who in the Confederacy: A Comprehensive, Illustrated Biographical Reference to More Than 1,000 of the Principal Confederacy Participants in the Civil* War. New York: Facts on File, 1988.

_____. *Who Was Who in the Union: A Comprehensive, Illustrated Biographical Reference to More Than 1,500 of the Principal Union Participants in the Civil War*. New York: Facts on File, 1988.

Starr, Stephen Z. *Jennison's Jayhawkers: A Civil War Cavalry Regiment and Its Commander*. Baton Rouge: Louisiana State University Press, 1974.

Sutherland, Daniel E., ed. *Reminiscences of a Private: William E. Bevens of the First Arkansas Infantry*. Fayetteville: University of Arkansas Press, 1992.

U.S. War Department. *The War of the Rebellion: A Compilation of the Official Records of the Union and Confederate Armies* 4 series, 70 vols. in 128 books and index. Washington: Government Printing Office, 1880-1901.

Warner, Ezra J. *Generals in Gray: Lives of the Confederate Commanders*. Baton Rouge: Louisiana State University Press, 1959.

Waugh, John C. *Sam Bell Maxey and the Confederate Indians*. Fort Worth, TX: Ryan Place Publishers, 1995.

Way, Frederick. *Way's Packet Directory, 1848-1994: Passenger Steamboats of the Mississippi River System Since the Advent of Photography in Mid-Continent America*. Athens: Ohio University Press, 1994.

Wiley, Bell Irvin. *The Common Soldier in the Civil War*. New York: Grosset & Dunlap, 1958.

ABOUT THE EDITOR

Tom Wing was a park ranger and historian for the National Park Service at the Fort Smith National Historic Site for eight years before leaving for the University of Arkansas—Fort Smith in August 2004 to teach in the new bachelor's degree program in history/historical interpretation.

He is chair of the West Central Arkansas War Heritage Trail and was appointed by the Arkansas Secretary of State to serve on the Advisory Team for the Bicentennial of the Louisiana Purchase. He has appeared on the Arkansas Educational Television Network and the History Channel.

A life-long resident of Fort Smith, he graduated from Northside High School and attended UA Fort Smith when it was Westark College. He then transferred to the University of Arkansas, Fayetteville, where he completed two bachelor's degrees. He also has a master's degree from the University of Oklahoma.

His hobbies and interests include hunting, living history, archeology, video games, forest fires and gardening. He lives with his wife Renee' and four sons, Jerry Allen, Justin, Jake, and Jackson in Crawford County, Arkansas, near Cove Creek, which Henry Strong crossed 13 times in December 1863, on his way to Fort Smith.

CPSIA information can be obtained
at www.ICGtesting.com
Printed in the USA
JSHW052004210722
28335JS00001B/37